23.12.13

Dear Hillary,

Wishing you a very

Christmas, and a wo———— — 14.

We hope to show you some of the

sights of Northumberland soon.

All our love,

Chris, Natalie + Paul.

Northumberland

Photography by Graeme Peacock
Text by Steve Newman

SANDERSON BOOKS LIMITED
NORTHUMBERLAND

First published in Great Britain in 2004
by Sanderson Books Limited.

Text and photographs copyright Steve Newman and Graeme Peacock, 2004
The moral right of Steve Newman and Graeme Peacock to be identified as the authors
of this work has been asserted in accordance with the Copyright, Designs and Patents Act of 1988.

ISBN 0954802403

Designed by Sokell Design / www.sokell.com
Photography by Graeme Peacock / www.graeme-peacock.com
Text by Steve Newman / www.stevenewman.co.uk
Editor: Catherine Bowen
Printed and Bound in Italy.
Set in Goudy Old Style.

Half-title page: Budle Bay near Bamburgh

Sanderson Books Limited
Front Street, Klondyke, Cramlington
Northumberland NE23 6RF

The authors would like to thank the following for their generous help and support, without which
the production of this book would not have been possible:

John Anderson, Audrey Atkin, Hugh Cantley, Clive Crossley, Howard Dawe, Adrian Irons, Katrina Porteous, Nick Renner
Thompson, The Alnwick Garden, The Coble & Keelboat Society, English Heritage, Ford & Etal Estates,
The National Trust, Northumberland County Council, Royal National Lifeboat Institution, The Vindolanda Trust.

CONTENTS

Yeavering Bell, The Cheviot Hills. Opposite: The Battle of Flodden Memorial

Northumberland

THE COUNTY

INTRODUCTION

Northumberland. The very word conjures up a feeling of open space and wide skies. A history that spans 450 million years would be impressive anywhere but Northumberland also has a character that is uniquely different from any other English county. In fact it is not too bold a statement to say that Northumberland is a country in its own right.

Sandwiched between Scotland and England Northumberland has drawn its lifeblood from both countries and at the same time influenced them enormously. If Scotland were to be described as red and England as yellow then Northumberland would be classified as orange. Northumberland too has its own bagpipes that have survived over the centuries and become a part of everyday life and its own unique tartan plaid that speaks immediately of history and pride.

Even the accent changes slowly as it moves northwards from the steep gorge of the River Allen to the sedately flowing Tweed. When this gradual metamorphosis from the lilt of Yorkshire to the lowland Scots brogue reaches Berwick it epitomises the nature of the county. Here the locals have an accent that is a mixture of Scottish and Northumbrian with both the football and rugby teams playing in the Scottish leagues!

It is this interlinking between her two neighbours that has more than anything else defined Northumberland today. The awful times of the border wars have resulted in more castles and fortified houses than any other county and introduced words such as 'blackmail' and 'hotfoot' to the English language.

Northumbrians are rightly proud of their county and why not? If it were not for them the trains of the world would not run on a standard gauge and the kipper would not have graced a million breakfast tables. Christianity, as we know it, owes an incredible debt to a small part time island off the coast and the landscaped grounds of Britain's grandest stately homes would be nowhere as magnificent.

Within Northumberland's borders you'll find England's largest reservoir situated in Britain's largest forest. But there is no overcrowding in this one of the country's larger counties, in fact the residential section of the phone book is less than half an inch thick! Within its pages names such as Turnbull, Dodds, Hindhaugh, Elliot, Nixon, Armstrong and Charlton still ring out as they have down the ages.

Yet physically Northumberland is a county of opposites. The green rolling, wooded hills of the south are in contrast to the high Cheviots where the curlew and grouse can be heard and where the wild goats still roam the hills, some two thousand years after their ancestors escaped from the Iron Age hill forts that dot the peaks.

To the south east the contrast could not be greater. Here in what was the industrial heartland, mining, engineering and other heavy industries dominated the landscape and peoples lives.

The legacy this industry left behind can be seen in the rows of terraced houses and the landscaped

Hadrian's Wall, near Gilsland

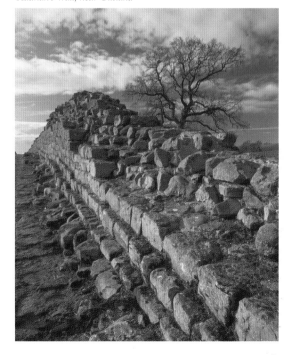

pit heaps as well as heard in the distinct twang of the locals in the former mining towns.

Northumberland's coastline is a different matter still where some of the finest beaches and best preserved sand dunes in Europe are to be found. The small fishing harbours that are dotted along the coast all tell silent stories of the time when herring was king as do the cobles that are to be found on the beaches. Unique in their design these sturdy craft reveal their Viking ancestry in their sleek clinker built lines.

Evidence of the violent past of Northumberland is never far away from your eyes and the coast is no exception with the great fortresses of Bamburgh and Dunstanburgh dominating the cliff tops. Yet move inland onto the Northern plain and there is evidence of even older human occupation with prehistoric cup and ring rock markings defying the wind and rain by still being visible after thousands of years.

This book is a proud celebration of Northumberland and through its pages you will dip into its history and the changes that have taken place over the centuries. There are interesting stories of the characters that have shaped its history and landscape, wonderful photographs of imposing houses and gardens, delightful villages waiting to be explored, peaceful beaches, castles and churches all set in the stunning scenery that is Northumberland. All of this is waiting to be discovered, treasured and enjoyed.

Upturned Boats, Lindisfarne

Sunset over Greenhead

Lindisfarne Village

Northumberland

A KINGDOM OF CASTLES

A KINGDOM OF CASTLES

It is almost impossible to mention Northumberland and not to think of castles. Some such as Bamburgh, Alnwick, Dunstanburgh and Lindisfarne are iconic, others such as Wark on the banks of the Tweed and Edlingham are virtually unknown to many of us yet have played a vital part in the history of these islands.

The turbulent past of the borders have resulted in more castles being built in Northumberland than any other county but the need for protection goes back even further in time.

The great Iron Age hill forts such as Dod Law, Humbleton and Yeavering Bell still have their surrounding ramparts. Yeavering is the largest hill fort in Northumberland and was a major population centre with some 130 huts inside. Beyond the main wall enclosing all of the double summit are additional defensive stone outworks on the east and west sides.

The steep, high slopes of the Cheviots offered natural protection to these early communities but when the Normans arrived their demands also included the necessity of a strategic position to control the surrounding countryside.

Many of these early sites however lacked the height and steep slopes of the hill fort so the Normans got over this defensive shortcoming by developing the motte and bailey castle. These mounds were mostly timber ramparts with very little stone, however they were so huge and effective that they have survived down to the present day.

Superb examples of this are to be seen at Elsdon, and Wark-on-Tweed where the earthworks are simply staggering when you stroll beside them. As time progressed some of these earlier castles were abandoned but in others the wooden buildings on the motte were replaced by a stone keep as can be seen at Alnwick and more dramatically, Warkworth.

Another instance of this can be seen at Harbottle in Upper Coquetdale, lying at an impotant crossing point on the Border where in 1541 its great stone keep was remodelled with a lower profile and fitted for light artillery pieces. A similar occurrence had happened earlier at Norham when small towers reinforced the keep with gun emplacements after a siege in 1513.

Some of the early castles followed a different pattern of construction such as Prudhoe, which was a 'ringwork' structure built of clay and stone. Others never even got finished such as Bywell, which has a very similar gatehouse to Bothal. These large gatehouses gradually replaced the keep, a defence fashion which reached its zenith at Dunstanburgh.

Other castles were chosen simply for their natural defensive position; Bamburgh, Dunstanburgh, Mitford and Aydon all spring to mind here although Bamburgh had the added factor of having been a fortress since the dark ages.

This need for a good defensive position continued into the Tudor period when the steep rock above Holy Island harbour was chosen as the site for a fort to protect the ships below. The castle at Lindisfarne was eventually transformed into a home as was Chillingham, but many others were demolished to make way for the grand houses of the local landowners.

Wallington Hall is built on the site of a castle owned by the Fenwick family whereas Berwick Castle was demolished by the Victorians to build the town's railway station.

Opposite: Warkworth Castle

BAMBURGH

Probably the most spectacularly sited of all our castles, Bamburgh stands guard over one of Northumberland's finest beaches. There has been a fortress here since 547 A.D. when a wooden palisade was built on the top of the crag.

Its name comes from Bebba, the wife of Ethelfrith who ruled Northumbria from 593 to 616 and it soon became known as Bebbanburgh. It remained an important fortress for the next 400 years, so much so, that the Normans, seeing it's importance, rebuilt it in stone.

The huge keep with walls some eleven feet thick was built in the reign of Henry I but the building we see today is a combination of restoration by Lord Crewe, Bishop of Durham, in the eighteenth century and then later by the First Lord Armstrong, the Victorian industrial magnate.

For a brief time in the twelfth century the castle was held by Henry, son of King David the first of Scotland, who at that time also held the Earldom of Northumberland until it was returned to the hands of Henry II in 1157.

The castle featured prominently in the Wars of the Roses but soon afterwards began to fall into neglect. In later years Bamburgh became, and still is, a family home and in fact the area around it makes for fascinating exploration. To the North the steep bank that marks the limit of the dunes is now thought by some archaeologists to be the original shoreline where boats were drawn up out of the water. To the south ancient gravesites have been

Above and opposite: Bamburgh Castle and Beach

found and indeed, if you look carefully, you can still make out signs of the original Bamburgh golf course.

On the north battlements is a conical tower standing alone which was in fact a windmill used for grinding corn for the local poor of the district. Below it is the water gate where Edward II entered the castle after the Battle of Bannockburn.

Bamburgh is also perhaps the most iconic of Northumberland's historical sites and often springs to mind first when people talk of the county. This is no surprise really due to its popularity with film and television producers for films such as Beckett and Braveheart.

WARKWORTH

Whether Warkworth is a castle with a village or a village with a castle is open to some debate. Trapped within a meander of the Coquet, the village still has a very medieval feel to it. The tree lined main street runs up to the castle, for so long the principle seat of the Percys.

Warkworth is thought to have been first erected around 1150 as a motte and bailey castle by Henry, Earl of Northumberland, the son of David I of Scotland.

In 1327 the castle had been besieged twice by the Scots and in 1332, because of its important strategic position, King Edward II, in London, granted it to the influential Percy family to provide a full-time defence against the Scots.

The castle was the birthplace of Harry Hotspur and saw much intrigue in the reign of Henry IV, so much so that scenes of the Shakespeare play of that title are set in Warkworth.

Pleasant riverside walks in the gorge are an option here and one of them upstream will take you to the ferry where you can cross the river and visit the fascinating Hermitage carved out of the rock.

The first hermit that is known was Thomas Barker who was appointed for life by the Earl of Northumberland in 1487. Spanning the river at the north of the village is a fourteenth century narrow stone bridge guarded by an even older gateway.

Whatever your impressions of Warkworth Castle there can be no doubt that it is very impressive and

Warkworth Castle and Village

is a superb example of how a fortification could also serve as a luxurious home.

Warkworth is a popular place on the tourist trail and there is little doubt the carpet of spring daffodils on the castle mound is one of the finest sights in Northumberland.

Art galleries, tea rooms and restaurants have also made the village one of the most sought after places to live in the county.

Warkworth market place and main street, looking towards the castle.

ALNWICK

Often referred to as 'The Windsor of the North' Alnwick Castle like so many others started life as wooden motte and bailey castle in the early eleventh century. Alnwick was heavily involved in the Border wars, indeed the Scottish King, William the Lion was captured here while riding too close to the castle in the fog. King John visited the castle on several occasions and eventually it was sold to the Percy family in 1309 and it remains the principal Percy seat to this day. The castle also saw action during the Wars of the Roses.

The first Duke of Northumberland in 1766 is responsible for the castle surviving through the ages, having changed his name to Percy, Sir Hugh Smithson set about re-ordering and modernising the vast estates and properties he had gained through his wife. By this time the castle was largely derelict, so an extensive programme of restoration was undertaken to convert the castle into a luxurious stately home required of the eighteenth century aristocracy.

The Alnwick Lion

As part of his modernisation programme, the Duke employed James Paine and Robert Adam, the latter bringing a romantic Gothic style to Alnwick, rather than the Neo-Classical style he is mostly remembered for. The fourth Duke, Algernon initiated major design works that resulted in the Renaissance Italianate style we see today. Another famous name associated with design is Capability Brown who worked on the grounds and produced the peaceful views of the landscape one can now see from the terrace, he also built to the north of the keep.

Each year on the pastures below the terrace, the Shrove Tuesday football match is played between the two parishes of Alnwick that consists of three periods of play and unlimited numbers on each side. Despite its proximity to the town centre, the castle is hidden from view, only seen clearly when approached from the north where it overlooks the River Aln. It has become a favourite location for film and television companies. Recent productions filmed here include Robin Hood Prince of Thieves and Harry Potter, and the castle was also the setting for the first series of Blackadder.

Alnwick Castle and Lion Bridge

AYDON

Robert de Reymes, a wealthy Suffolk merchant, began construction of Aydon Castle in 1296, and in doing so created what is now one of the finest examples of a medieval manor house in England.

Aydon was built at the end of an unusually long era of peace in the borders and as the building is naturally defended on one side by the steep valley of the Cor Burn it was originally unfortified. However, unfortunately for Robert, no sooner had he finished his new home than the Scots began raiding again throughout Northumberland.

In 1305, he was granted a licence to fortify his property and set about improving the defences with the addition of the battlements and a circuit of curtain walls. However these fortifications didn't stop the Scots from sacking the property in 1315 and 1346.

Over the centuries the manor house had numerous owners, many of whom lived elsewhere and leased the property to tenants and because of this the manor was left largely unchanged. The only significant modifications were made during a mid-sixteenth century renovation and a seventeenth century conversion to a farm. The buildings remained in use as a farm until 1966 when it was entrusted to the Ministry of works by the then owners, the Blacketts of Matfen.

The castle's remarkably intact survival is nothing short of incredible and can be attributed to the later conversion to a farmhouse and now, thanks to English Heritage, it still provides a splendid impression of how a minor baron may have lived during the reign of Edward I.

Like many castles Aydon's fascination is in the scars of former buildings still visible on the walls. This is particularly evident in the external flight of stone steps leading up to the west end of the Great Hall, above them, quite clearly seen, is the line of a lean-to covering.

Aydon Castle

BELSAY

For over five hundred years, apart from a short break in the fourteenth century, Belsay Castle was the principal seat of the Middleton family. The Middletons were an important family, indeed one of them was Lord Chancellor of England in the thirteenth century.

The original castle was essentially a typical tower house and is thought to have been built about 1360. This tower house is built on an almost square plan and is over 18 metres high, it is especially noteworthy for the huge sections overhanging the corners and the protruding machicolations from which hot water and rocks could be thrown on any attackers below.

In the early seventeenth century Thomas Middleton built a two storied range still visible today. The Jacobean mullioned windows demonstrate clearly the changing times when defence was no longer the main factor in Northumberland buildings, but that light and a high degree of comfort were now essential for a residence of the gentry.

However, not much remains of the west wing built nearly 100 years later in 1717 by his descendant Sir John Middleton. An engraving of 1728 exists that shows the balanced building fronted by formal gardens, which have now vanished, but the ha-ha still remains.

In 1795 Sir Charles Middleton was obliged to change his name to Monck to inherit an estate in Lincolnshire. From 1804-1806 he spent his honeymoon abroad where he was greatly influenced by the art and culture of the ancient Greeks. On his return he decided to build a Grecian house on his estate and the family subsequently left Belsay Castle and moved into Belsay Hall on Christmas Day 1817.

Edward I was once a guest here but during the reign of his son, Edward II, the castle was used by Sir Gilbert de Middleton as a base to ravage the borders with a large force. It is said only Norham, Bamburgh and Alnwick held out against him.

Belsay Castle

EDLINGHAM

Edlingham Castle

Castles are usually built on a dominating site where they can control large areas of the countryside and that at the same time offers them good defensive properties. It comes as something of a surprise then, that Edlingham Castle lies at the bottom of a valley between Alnwick and Rothbury standing next to Edlingham Burn.

John de Edlingham built a large two-storey Hall House in a moated enclosure in the mid thirteenth century. In 1296 the property was taken over by Sir William de Felton who added a palisade inside the moat and a gatehouse on the north side.

Sir William Felton constructed a fine hall house around 1298 and the most notable feature of the castle is a three-storey residential tower off the south side of the house. It stands up to 30.5 metres high and has a spectacular fireplace. After 1420 ownership passed to the Hastings family until 1519 and then to the Swinburnes. These two families did not need the defensive capabilities of a castle, and until its final abandonment in 1650 the property was used as a farm with several of the buildings converted to house livestock. The castle is in the care of English Heritage.

Edlingham also has a fine Norman church with one of the few Norman porches in the county. To the east of the castle is the viaduct that carried the railway line of the Alnwick to Cornhill branch. The viaduct is interesting as it was one of the first to be built with a curve in it.

The village of Edlingham lies beside the castle in a narrow green vale below the wild heather covered moors. It is best viewed from the high point on the Alnwick road below Corby's Crags which also gives a marvellous view northwards out towards the Cheviots. Its church is a simple rugged structure that seems to blend in so completely with its surroundings with its porch being one of the few Norman examples in Northumberland. The wide chancel is also of Norman work but its most impressive feature is the north aisle with round arches on round pillars and beautiful carving.

Another ecclesiastical building is to be found in the parish of Edlingham in the small settlement of Bolton. It holds a chapel of ease and although it was considerably restored in the nineteenth century, the foundation is ancient, and some Norman work survives. A leper hospital was founded to the north of Bolton in 1227 under the terms of a licence granted by the Prior of Durham who held it until the Dissolution and the chapel was probably connected in some way to this.

NORHAM

Sited about halfway between Berwick and Coldstream, Norham Castle is one of the most impressive military fortresses in northern England and guarded a strategic ford over the Tweed.

The castle was founded by The Prince Bishop, Ranulph Flambard of Durham, as the administrative centre or "Northern Homestead" for his most northern lands in 1121. Frequent raids by the Scots forced a rebuilding in stone and Hugh de Puiset, the then Bishop, built extensively between 1157 and 1170, including the construction of the Great Tower which had two storeys with a basement and still stands today reaching over 27.5 metres feet high in places.

The castle fell to the Scots in 1513 when James IV bombarded the walls with 'Mons Meg', a huge cannon now in Edinburgh Castle. However the battle of Flodden was fought a week or so later where James and the flower of his nobility perished.

The castle features in Sir Walter Scott's 'Marmion', named after a Lincolnshire knight who led a sortie from the castle in one of its many sieges.

Norham castle was also painted by Turner from one of the gravel islands you can see in the river below. Recent survey work by English Heritage has shown that the medieval castle occupies the site of a much earlier fortification. This may be a prehistoric hill fort, perhaps as much as 3,000 years old. In fact, the earthwork was first noticed in the nineteenth century and interpreted as a Roman fort, but this suggestion was forgotten over time. If English Heritage is correct in the dating of this rampart, then Norham could well boast the site of the largest Iron Age hill fort in Northumberland.

The attractive village of Norham lies below the castle with its triangular green and long wide street of cottages. On the green stands the pinnacled market cross set on a base of six thirteenth century steps.

Norham Castle

DUNSTANBURGH

Dunstanburgh Castle

Dunstanburgh castle is unusual in as much as it was not built on the site of a previous fortification. The site was deliberately chosen as it gives protection on two sides by the sheer 30.5 metres of cliff face and the sea.

Dunstanburgh was built between 1313 and 1325 for Thomas Earl of Lancaster, nephew of King Edward II. A cousin of the King, Lancaster was second only to him in wealth but eventually he rebelled and was finally executed at Pontefract in 1322.

The outstanding feature of the castle is its massive gatehouse, which guarded the entrance to the largest area of any Northumberland castle. This offered good protection to local villagers, their animals and possessions in the event of a raid from the Scots. The castle was used to supply men and horses for Edward II's invasion of Scotland.

In 1362, John of Gaunt, fourth son of Edward III, inherited the castle and had the great gatehouse converted into a keep. His son, Henry of Bolingbroke, inherited in 1399 and subsequently usurped the throne as Henry IV. Dunstanburgh thus became a royal castle and a Lancastrian stronghold during the Wars of the Roses when it suffered terribly from cannon fire.

When first captured its Lancastrian commander Sir Ralph Percy was allowed to stay but he soon reverted to the Lancastrian cause and the castle underwent another siege and surrendered soon

after. In the first quarter of the sixteenth century much stone and materials were taken from the castle to repair the more strategic fortress of Wark on Tweed. Despite its ruinous state however, Dunstanburgh presents a formidable and imposing sight when viewed from afar. Today it is owned by English Heritage.

Perhaps the castle is at its most majestic in stormy weather as when Turner painted it on one of his trips here. It is a just tribute to its builders that so much of the castle still stands today.

Perched on an outcrop of that same Whin Sill where one finds Hadrian's Wall and Bamburgh Castle, Dunstanburgh stands on equal footing with them as one of the major icons of Northumberland.

Dunstanburgh Castle

MITFORD

Five sided keeps in castles were extremely rare. So rare in fact that there was only one in England and that was at Mitford. The site is a strong one guarded by the ravine of the Wansbeck on one side and by steep slopes on the others and this must have been what appealed to the Norman builders.

It's thought that in the early medieval period Mitford's fords probably offered a better river crossing for travellers than nearby Morpeth's. This is why Mitford became a place of much greater importance than its neighbour.

Mitford's name is derived from the site's location between two fords over the rivers Font and Wansbeck and the church dates from 1135. The village was granted a charter for a market and became a borough some 50 years at least before Morpeth.

There is a small cross cut into the parapet of the bridge near Snuff Mill. It commemorates the Rev. Isaac Nelson, Admiral Nelson's uncle, who was vicar of Mitford until on 20th March 1772 he drowned trying to cross the 'steppy' stones above the bridge.

There were Mitfords here before the conquest and after 1066 a Mitford heiress was given in marriage to one Sir Richard Bertram and the estate remained in the family's hands until the late 1990s.

Other members of the family established themselves elsewhere including the Exbury branch, headed by Lord Redesdale, which included the

Mitford Castle

famous Mitford sisters. Bordered on three sides by the Wansbeck, Mitford Hall was built by Dobson in 1828 when the old manor house was pulled down and the pele tower left intact.

Between the castle and the Hall is the church which still displays some Norman and medieval features. The tall tower and spire are of mid Victorian origin but much of the interior including the lovely south arcade is of medieval origin.

It is however to the ruins of the castle that the eye is drawn. It is difficult to imagine when standing in the original gateway the violence that took place here when, after Bannockburn, the Bishop of Durham was rescued by forces loyal to the crown. William de Felton slew the porters in the gateway when bringing the ransom money and his forces rushed in to secure the castle.

BERWICK BARRACKS

Being a citizen of Berwick in the early years of the eighteenth century was not much fun if you were one of the unfortunate souls who had soldiers from the local garrison billeted in your home. It was considered normal for soldiers in the town to be lodged in inns or even private houses and this caused friction between the townspeople and the military.

Complaints to the Government became so strong that it was decided to construct the first purpose-built barracks to be erected and work began in Ravensdown in 1717 shortly after the suppression of the Jacobite uprisings.

Although often attributed to Vanbrugh, they were actually designed by Nicholas Hawksmoor and completed by 1725. They contained accommodation for 600 men and 36 officers, in two three-storey blocks facing each other across the drill square.

The third block, opposite the entrance, was erected in 1739 and was the site of the store block and gunpowder magazine. It now houses the Berwick Borough Museum which holds a sizeable part of the world famous Burrell Collection.

The barrack block on the western side of the parade square is still in military use, and is therefore not open to the public, by both the town's cadet forces and visiting units. The east block now houses a museum on the development of the British Army and how soldiers lived when it was first built as well as the Regimental Museum of

Berwick Barracks

The Kings Own Scottish Borderers.

Behind this block is the old gymnasium that now holds exhibitions of contemporary art. Each year the barracks plays host to a military tattoo with massed pipes and drums, military bands and other displays.

The Barracks are in the care of English Heritage who organise a series of historical events throughout the year as well as maintaining the fabric of the building. An excellent overall view of the buildings can be obtained from the town walls to the south of Cowgate.

ETAL

Standing beside the River Till, Etal castle guarded the crossing for the main road to Cornhill and the castle at Wark. The castle started out as a three-storey tower house built by the Manners family, but the close proximity to the border made it exceptionally vulnerable to attack.

In 1341, the owner, Robert Manners, was granted a licence to fortify his home. It was probably not just the threat of the Scots however that made him do this as the family had a bitter running feud with the Herons of Ford Castle who had fortified their home a few years earlier.

The feud came to a head in 1427 when it was claimed that John Manners, heir to the Etal estate, had slain William Heron of Ford and one of his companions.

William's widow complained that her husband had been "maliciously slayne" by John Manners, but in defence John stated that William had come to Etal with an armed force and had led a "gret assaut made in shotyng of arrowes and strykyng with swerdes." Judgement went against John Manners however who had to pay 250 marks to the widow of William Heron and in addition had to pay for 500 masses to be said for the soul her husband.

In 1513 the castle succumbed to the army of James IV of Scotland during his invasion of England. James was killed nearby at the Battle of Flodden and the Scottish cannon was brought back to the castle to be stored.

In 1549 the castle was ceded to the Crown, perhaps in an attempt to reduce the neglect of what was after all a strategic border castle. The castle is in the care of English Heritage.

Today the castle can now be reached by a miniature railway running from Heatherslaw Mill. Originally there was also a bridge across the River Till, a little further upstream from the ford, and the weir that is so beloved by today's canoeists.

Etal Castle

CHILLINGHAM

In the thirteenth century Chillingham Castle existed as little more than a tower, but just 100 years later in 1344, Sir Thomas Grey was granted a licence to crenellate his property. He built a quadrangular castle with four corner towers and an inner courtyard.

A curtain wall was built around the castle grounds, but this has now mostly disappeared, although some remains can be seen at the end of the present Italian Garden. This was the beginning of the fortress that has, quite remarkably, survived to become an inhabited family home today.

In 1590 alterations were made to the castle, which included moving the main entrance to its present position, in preparation for the royal visit of King James VI of Scotland on his journey south to his English coronation.

Further alterations were carried out in the seventeenth century when the famous architect and designer Inigo Jones was employed to redesign the castle to give better accommodation and a greater degree of comfort.

The last major works were carried out around the middle of the nineteenth century when a new service wing was constructed, and the castle grounds were laid out. These included the creation of the Italian garden which turned the castle into a stately home with landscaped gardens.

Chillingham is one of the most haunted castles in the country and frequently hosts television and

Chillingham Castle

film crews carrying out documentary and research programmes into its spectral inhabitants. Amongst the ghosts is Lady Mary Berkely whose rustling dress can still be heard along the corridors of the castle and stairs with her progress accompanied by chilling blast of air.

The wild Chillingham White Cattle have now been here for over 700 years. The cattle are the sole survivors of their species to remain uncrossed with other domestic breeds and are thus a living part of Northumberland's history.

Warkworth Castle

Northumberland

HOUSES AND GARDENS

HOUSES AND GARDENS

As the border wars and the days of the reivers gradually drew to a close, the last recorded skirmish between Scots and English took place at Crookham in 1678, a change began in the architecture of Northumberland.

No longer were solid walls and defensive capability considered the priority and nowhere else in the county is this exemplified in one visual glance than at Belsay Castle.

The original castle was essentially a typical tower house, standing next to it is the early seventeenth century manor house with Jacobean mullioned windows demonstrating clearly the changing times that light and a high degree of comfort were now essential for a residence of the gentry. Not much remains of the west wing built nearly 100 years later or the formal gardens, which have now vanished, but the ha-ha still remains.

Another fine example of this is Chillingham where gradually the castle evolved into a stately home, so much so that the jousting yard became a fine Italianate garden. This conversion of fortress to home reached its pinnacle with Alnwick Castle and to a lesser extent, with many of the pele towers such as Craster, Fourstones and Kirkharle where the ancient fabric was incorporated into a manor house.

Many land owners however wanted to build their own house away from the site of the castle as with Belsay and gradually the large country house we now see today came into being. Not all these houses were built by the descendents of the border reiver families. A new class was evolving who earned their fortune from agriculture, mining and other industries.

Wallington is an example of this phenomena. Formerly a residence of the Fenwick's, it was Sir Wiliam Blackett, a wealthy mine owner and merchant from Newcastle upon Tyne who set about building the present house. Down the years his family carried on improving the house and estate including indulging in the fashion for vast landscapes to be created in the grounds.

Here at Wallington, as at other houses, Lancelot 'capability' Brown left his mark. He was born at Kirkhale and went to school at Cambo so it is no surprise he worked here.

This fashion for landscaped grounds can be seen at Alnwick where Hulne Park is a prime example with its vistas and viewing point at Brizlee Tower. At the same time the Folly came into fashion with one of the most striking being Rothley Castle.

It is said by many that the very pinnacle of the country house design is to be found in Northumberland. Designed by Sir John Vanburgh, who was responsible for Blenheim Palace and Castle Howard, Seaton Delaval Hall may not be as large as the latter but its compact and powerful design is regarded as being of a superior nature.

Like many of the grand houses Seaton Delaval suffered from fire and by being occupied by troops in the war years. The latter was also suffered by Belford Hall which has now been tastefully converted into flats, a fate which has also occurred at Callaley Castle.

Towards the end of the nineteenth century new industries brought new wealth and as a result The first Lord Armstrong, the son of a corn merchant, was with his great wealth able to build the magnificent 'Palace of the Magician' at Cragside.

Around the same time other men were making their fortune in publishing, Edward Hudson, the owner of Country Life, bought Lindisfarne Castle in 1902 and with the help of the great Edward Lutyens set about converting it into a home.

With some of the great houses their grounds have been converted and landscaped yet again but this time as golf courses such as at Matfen, Slaley, Linden Hall and Longhirst.

At the same time the evolution of garden design continues a pace in the county with the creation of the Duchess of Northumberland's Alnwick Garden. An amazing example of twenty-first cetury technology blending with the horticultural skills developed over the centuries.

Opposite - The Grand Cascade, Alnwick Garden

THE ALNWICK GARDEN

As the fashion for gardens escalated, the 1st Duke of Northumberland laid down the first garden at Alnwick, he also employed Capability Brown to landscape the parkland adjoining the castle grounds. The current site, about 100 metres from Alnwick Castle, is believed to be one of the largest walled gardens in the world and is enclosed in 250 year old walls.

An archaeological survey revealed traces of seven previous gardens dating back to the eighteenth century. Prior to The Alnwick Garden which opened in 2002 however, the gardens were at their most complete in the mid-nineteenth century when the fourth Duke called upon William Andrews Nesfield to create stunning new gardens in the Italian Renaissance style.

By the end of the nineteenth century the gardens were at their grandest with yew hedges in topiary, a double avenue of limes, acres of flower garden, five grape houses, five pine houses and a conservatory. Underneath were vast underground tunnels which provided hot air for the greenhouses, the heat being produced by large underground coal-fired furnaces, but the twentieth century saw the gardens fall into disrepair.

Historical features are still visible in the new Alnwick Garden such as the two large earth banks that run down either side of the Grand Cascade. These were first constructed in the garden of the 1850's and became the starting point for the vision

The Rose Garden, The Alnwick Garden

of The Alnwick Garden. The main axis of the Cascade also runs down to the existing viewing platform which was the site of the 1860 pavilion and is the site of the twenty-first century Alnwick Garden Pavilion.

An early eighteenth century lead sculpture of a fox sitting atop a fruit-filled urn decorated with masks depicting the four seasons and supported by monkeys can also still be seen in the present garden. Interestingly this sculpture never appeared in any of the former gardens but holds its place admirably in the centre of the Rose Garden.

ALNWICK
ORNAMENTAL GARDEN

The continuity of history is ever present in Northumberland. Inside The Alnwick Garden is a smaller walled garden accessible through three inter-linked stone arches. Here you'll find three 500-year-old wrought iron Venetian gates spanning the arched entrance into the part of The Garden known as the Ornamental Garden.

The visual interest of this garden comes from the use of interaction between light and shade and the grey and green foliage. To complement this, flowers and fruit are found in a delicate planting pattern, this visual play is enhanced above ground level by the creation of beautiful lacework in the air, known as pleaching, using delicate crab apples.

At the centre of this garden is a pool from which a series of pebbled rills flow leading you to other delightful areas. Pergolas surrounding the pool are covered in vines and rambling plants and boxwood-edged beds house a collection of bedding roses surrounded by delphiniums.

Thus the Ornamental Garden offers a total contrast to the starkness of the Cascade. Its here one can enjoy the colours and scents provided by over 16,500 plants designed to flower at different times of the year creating bands of colour. At the perimeter is a wide herbaceous border full of musk hybrids, tree peonies, shrubs, and solitary ornamental trees with rose-covered arbours in each corner.

The planting scheme of the Ornamental Garden is designed to draw the eye of the visitor through it and offer intrigue and delight. Attractively designed 'oversized' benches of Douglas Fir, which complement the scale of The Garden, are placed throughout the Ornamental Garden and two dovecotes attract birds to offer a dimension of sound to this peaceful place.

The strength of the Ornamental Garden is to be found in its colour and individuality. Yet, at the same time, it is an integral part of the entire structure that is the garden.

Alnwick Ornamental Garden

BRIZLEE TOWER

In the scheme of eighteenth century landscape, planning vistas were very important. In particular the creation of specific views, centred on a folly was considered a vital factor of any large estate parkland. The landscape was often laid out so that it was best appreciated from a specific viewpoint with the folly attracting the eye. Hulne Park in Alnwick has such an example in Brizlee Tower built by Robert Adam for the first Duke of Northumberland in 1781.

This elaborate ornamental tower in the Gothic style was built as a viewing platform to observe the park and indeed can be seen from miles around. The tower has six stages, the lowest of which has a veranda and the highest a balcony, above which the whole is capped by a cast iron fire basket.

There is some speculation that the Duke himself may have designed the tower as it bears the inscription: "Circumspice! Ego omnia ista sum dimensus; Mei sunt ordines, Mea descriptio Multae Etiam istarum arborum Mea manu sunt satae", which translates as: "Look around! I have measured out all these things; they are my orders, it is my planting; many of these trees have even been planted by my hand".

The three thousand acres of Hulne Park have a lot more to offer including three species of deer which now live within its boundaries namely fallow, red and roe.

The river Aln runs through the park past Hulne Priory, founded in 1240 and built on a green hill above a wooded bend of its course, and eventually past the magnificent gatehouse of the abbey before flowing past the castle and on to the sea.

Brizlee Tower still serves a function for the local people today as during charity clay pigeon shoots its balcony is used to launch some of the most challenging clays to be found.

The Brizlee Tower, in Hulne Park, Alnwick

CRAGSIDE

Cragside House and Gardens

Situated on a crag high above Rothbury the house at Cragside was mainly designed by Richard Norman Shaw and developed from a lodge by Lord Armstrong for shooting or fishing parties. Shaw started building in 1869 in three separate building campaigns and developed a house with aspects of German, French and Old English styles.

The house was often referred to as the 'Palace of the Magician' as it had hot and cold running water, fire alarms, central heating, telephones and a Turkish bath, but most remarkable of all, it was the first house in the world to be lit by hydroelectricity. So popular did the house become that the Prince and Princess of Wales visited in 1884 when it was finally completed.

Water was pumped up some 70 metres above the house and then flowed down to power the devices that were so necessary to Victorian country house life, including a spit in the kitchen and a passenger lift.

Whilst Shaw continued with the house, Armstrong and his wife, who was also a keen and accomplished gardener, set about planting and developing the bleak moorland. This included planting up to seven million trees and bushes to cover the bare hillside and create the 1000-acre forest garden you can explore today.

Lakes were created and azaleas and rhododendrons were planted to give the estate the magnificent colours and stunning displays that people flock to see and is justly famous for today.

Around and below the house is one of Europe's largest rock gardens formed by hundreds of large round boulders that were manhandled into position by local workmen. Whilst across the valley is the terraced garden where exotic fruits for consumption in the house were nurtured throughout the year in glasshouses. The house is now in the care of the National Trust.

Besides the house the estate contains other lesser known buildings that hold both a technical and historic interest. This includes the Tumbleton Ram House, situated just beneath Tumbleton Lake. Built around 1866 it housed the hydraulic engine that drove the pumps to the resevoir 70 metres above the house.

In front of the house is the majestic steel footbridge that crosses the ravine and was probably built in Armstrong's Elswick works.

LINDISFARNE

If you were to compile a list of icons of Northumberland then the castle on Holy Island would be very close to the top of that list. Built around 1550 the castle was intended to protect the harbour, at that time an extremely strategic and important port, from raids by the Scots. It suffered an unsuccessful siege of six weeks by Royalist troops during the Civil War. However two Jacobite supporters captured the castle in 1715 when Lancelot Errington and his nephew Mark hoisted the Jacobite flag and waited for reinforcements. Unfortunately the only troops who arrived were loyalist soldiers from Berwick and the Erringtons were soon captured and retired to Berwick gaol from which they almost immediately escaped!

In 1902 the castle was bought by Edward Hudson who employed Sir Edward Lutyens the greatest architect of the day, to restore the derelict castle. For the next nine years the work continued and resulted in an amazing conglomeration of styles and effects. The entrance to the castle no longer has its protective parapet but the portcullis can still be seen as you pass through.

To walk around the interiors of the castle is an experience in itself, as rooms seem to change from a comfortable warm home to a medieval living and back again with a series of shapes and styles constantly emerging. Lutyens genius was to construct the rooms and passages in such a manner that they seem almost to have been carved from the living rock. One of the gems of the castle is in fact some two hundred yards to the north and often ignored by visitors. Here lies the walled garden designed by Gertude Jekyll with a beautiful selection of plants and paths now maintained along with the castle by The National Trust.

Constructed of stone taken from the Priory, the most interesting recent feature in the castle's history has been the re-facing of north-facing walls, which took place in 1997 and used yak hair in the render. To the east of the castle are found three upturned boats, now used as storage, that were once part of the island's herring fleet. Whilst below are the huge lime kilns, some of the largest and best preserved in existence.

Opposite and right: Lindisfarne Castle

PRESTON TOWER

Like most pele towers in Northumberland, Preston Tower has seen its fair share of trouble in its 600 year history. The tower was built in 1392 and mentioned as one of 78 existing in Northumberland in 1415, the year of Agincourt. At this time Robert Harbottle, who had been Sheriff of the County and Constable of Dunstanburgh Castle a few miles away, held it. A later tenant had to promise to thatch the roof with "hather flags and strawe". Some 200 years later on another owner Guiscard Harbottle was slain at the Battle of Flodden fighting the Scots.

It was originally an oblong tower with four corner turrets and walls some over 2 metres thick. Unusually for pele towers, not only the basement of the southwest tower is vaulted but so is the first floor.

Following the Union of the Crowns peace descended on the Borders and in 1603 two of the original four towers were pulled down to provide building material for the nearby farm buildings on the estate.

When the present neo-classical early nineteenth century house was built alongside, the owners of the tower constructed the north wall and a striking clock was installed in the centre of the tower. The tower is three storeys high and has the typical vaulted rooms along with a guardroom and prison on the ground floor, the first floor had a living room and bedroom. Even today the tower is surrounded by elements of Northumberland's turbulent past. To the east lies Brunton Airfield that saw service during the second world war along with other stations in Northumberland such as Acklington and Milfield.

Almost equidistant to the west is the small village of Ellingham. Here at Ellingham Hall lived the Haggerstons, who were secret supporters of the Jacobite cause. When the Baronet of the day was obliged to lend support to convey 'Butcher' Cumberland to Berwick from Belford he bribed the driver to overturn the coach.

Preston Tower

LANGLEY CASTLE

The gardens at Langley Castle are not as extensive as one would expect. Now a private hotel the castle is remarkable in that it has hardly changed since it was built in 1364. The castle was the stronghold of the Lucy family but after only 50 years it was gutted by fire, perhaps on the orders of Henry IV as a punishment for the revolt in the north which the husband of Langley's heiress, Henry Percy, took part in, and though it passed through many hands no one made it habitable until 1882.

That year Cadwallader Bates, the noted Northumbrian historian, bought the property and made it his life's ambition to restore it. Because none of the intervening generations had added their period influences to the architecture it looks pretty much as it did 600 years ago.

The site is a strong one for a castle, as it is built between two burns. The foundations do not go below ground as they lie on a base of huge boulders. The two metre walls were placed in the form of an oblong, with a tower at each corner. Adjoining one of these on the east side was the entrance turret where the small portcullis could be let down by a rope passing through a boss in the vaulting shaped like man's head.

The Garderobe Tower originally had a spiral stone staircase and the garderobes (Medieval toilets) are now exposed and well preserved. Langley had high standards of sanitation for its day, with wooden seats supported by the stone lips on either side of the chutes.

Sadly Cadwallader Bates died in 1902, only a few years into his restoration project, but his wife Josephine realised his dream and even built a Catholic chapel in the South East Tower. After she died in 1932, the castle remained empty until it was used as a barracks during the Second World War, and then a girls' school and eventually became converted to the hotel it is today. To the east running just on the other side of the road to Whitfield is the disused railway line that carried the lead ore from Allendale to Hexham.

Langley Castle

WALLINGTON HALL

If one wanted to see an encapsulated history of Northumberland, one could do worse than visit Wallington. Scenes from Northumberland's legends and history adorn the walls of the central hall, with that wealth of detail that the Pre-Raphaelites are justly famous for.

Wallington is unusual as there is no sweeping drive and gateway up to the house, rather it sits close to the road with the front garden gently lapping up towards the front façade. At the bottom of this garden four stone griffin heads sit on the lawn. They were transported by ship to Newcastle upon Tyne from London and are said to have adorned one of the city's original medieval gateways.

Beneath the present house the cellars are all that remains of the castle that once stood here as did a Tudor mansion both being replaced by a square house in 1688. The Fenwicks held the estate from the Middle Ages until Sir John Fenwick sold it to Sir William Blackett in 1688.

Drastic improvements were made to this house in the eighteenth century when Danial Garret was employed by Sir Walter Calverly Blackett to drastically transform the house. At the same time Lancelot 'Capability' Brown, who went to school nearby in Cambo, became involved with the landscaping of the grounds.

In 1846 Sir Walter Trevelyn inherited the

Above and opposite: Wallington Hall and Gardens

house. He was man of great curiosity and gained a reputation as a botanist and geologist. His wife Pauline was an accomplished painter and friendly with the Pre-Raphaelites, Ruskin and Millais, who both visited the house.

Sir Walter had several gifted scientists amongst his friends, including John Fox-Talbot the father of photography.

The extensive grounds of Wallington contain woodland walks and ornamental ponds. The walled garden is justly famous and contains a rockery and a fascinating conservatory holding enormous fuscias and climbing plants.

SEATON DELAVAL HALL

Seaton Delaval Hall

Hubert De La Val, related by marriage to William the Conqueror was granted lands in Northumberland in the late eleventh century and it is from him that the area and family take their name.

Some six hundred years later his descendant Admiral George Delaval inherited the estate. The Admiral was appointed British Envoy to Portugal and Morocco with responsibility for buying materials and supplies for the British Army, and as a result had amassed a considerable personal fortune.

On arrival he looked at the crumbling old Delaval manor house in Seaton Burn Dene and decided at once to build a family seat on a far grander scale, thus in 1718 he employed John Vanburgh to design it. With Blenheim Palace and Castle Howard already to his name, this was to be Vanburgh's last and perhaps most memorable creation to which he devoted the last years of his life.

Sadly, before the palatial Palladian mansion was completed the Admiral met his death after falling from his horse. The hall was badly devastated by a huge fire in 1822 that nearly destroyed the central block, when the smoke settled just two rooms survived.

The hall has a magnificent stable block and is renowned for its 1947 garden, created by James Russell, finely made with a topiary parterre, pond and fountain.

The Church of Our Lady, Seaton, is the Parish Church built about the end of the eleventh century by Guy de Laval and consecrated in 1102 by Bishop Flambard of Durham. For over 700 years the Church remained the private chapel of the Delaval family and their staff.

On the death, in 1814, of the last male Delaval the estate passed, by marriage, to a Norfolk family. Sir Jacob Henry Astley of Kings Lynn, inherited the property and in 1817 it passed to his son, Jacob, who revived the family title of Baron Hastings in 1841. Finally in 1891 the church was presented to the Church of England for ever and became the Parish Church of the Parish of Delaval.

BELSAY HALL

Belsay Hall, and Quarry Gardens, right

When Sir Charles Monck built Belsay Hall he also demolished the original medieval village of Belsay and moved it out of sight further to the east.

The house is regarded as being of European importance with its square mathematically calculated dimensions and Neo-classical appearance. This is helped by the magnificent Doric portico and Doric frieze that runs around the building that contrasts completely with the stark honey coloured limestone walls. Inside the Hall, the rooms are set out like those of a Greek or Roman house around a top-lit central space and these are surrounded by superimposed colonnades.

Sir Charles dramatically transformed the quarry from which the stone was taken to build his new home into perhaps the jewel of Belsay, the 11 acre quarry garden. The garden is comprised of a microclimate of corridors, ravines and pinnacles dotted with vines and ferns, where exotic and rare plants grow, including palms and eucryphias.

In the late nineteenth and early twentieth Century Sir Charles's grandson Sir Arthur Middleton extended the garden and introduced the rhododendrons and other plants new to Britain at the time.

There are also terraced gardens close to the house with deep mixed borders, a magnolia terrace of multi colours, a rhododendron garden, a winter garden with heathers and a 27.5 metre high Douglas Fir planted in 1830. The sunken lawns are today used for croquet tournaments.

The Middletons left Belsay in 1962 and the house with its impressive stable block and outbuildings is now in the care of English Heritage.

KIRKHARLE

In 1336 Sir Wiliam de Harle founded a chantry and rebuilt the little church at Kirkharle. Today this church still stands and is particularly noted for its beautifully squared and jointed masonry.

The estate belonged to the Loraine family, one of whom is remembered in a standing stone to the northwest of the present courtyard. In 1483 the unfortunate Robert Loraine when returning from church alone, was ambushed by a party of Scots, who, not content with merely killing him, cut up his body and sent it home in his horse's saddlebags!

The other claim to fame of Kirkharle is that it was here in 1715 that Lancelot 'Capability' Brown was born and also here that he started his career as a landscape gardener in the employment of Sir William Loraine.

Today the courtyard where Brown worked holds a series of studios for crafts people and an exhibition concerning the great man. The old pele tower of the de Harles is still intact though it is doubtful whether any one from those times would recognise it as it now forms part of a house, built in the early English style with embattled towers and a great front bay.

In 1541 it was described as being "in good reparation", by then it had passed in to the hands of the Fenwicks and later the Aynsleys. The house eventually passed into the hands of the Anderson family who still live there today.

To the south of Kirkharle is the village of

Kirkharle

Capheaton. The names means the 'chief village of a district' and there are a wide range of archaeological and historical sites in the area. In 1543 the outlawed Charltons of Tynedale led the Elywhites, Nixons and Crosiers of Liddesdale to burn the village.

A hoard of silver vessels and coins were found here in the eighteenth century and several items are now displayed in the British Museum. As well as this discovery, the village has also been the location of another rare find, an Anglo Saxon hanging bowl that is now in the Museum of Antiquities, Newcastle upon Tyne.

HOWICK HALL

Prior to 1780 a small pele tower was to be found where Howick Hall now stands. The house was rebuilt after a fire in 1926 but it is the gardens at Howick that are its glory. This grand eighteenth century house has terrace and woodland gardens and was originally based on the transition idea, running from terrace to lawn to woodland garden.

In particular the gardens are renowned for the extensive grounds that offer a riot of spring bulbs, a woodland garden with lovely azaleas, camellias, magnolias and rhododendrons in spring, whilst in autumn cercidiphyllum and maples give a display of brilliant colour.

Howick has been the home of the Grey family since the fourteenth century. The best known member of the family was the second Earl Grey, who was the Prime Minister responsible for passing the Great Reform Bill of 1832. As a result of this parliamentary constituencies of roughly equal size and the one man, one vote, electoral system we now have today.

His monument stands at the top of Grey Street in Newcastle upon Tyne and many a tired person has been refreshed by a pot of tea that bears his name. The Estate has now passed through descendants to the present Lord Howick of Glendale. He planted most of the old hardwoods and also created the Long Walk, a dene that starts at the east end of the woodland garden and winds down to the sea for

Howick Hall

one and a half miles following Howick Burn.

Here you will find one of the finest stretches of the Northumberland coast. The public footpath from the mouth of the Howick Burn runs alongside Howick Haven and past the cave known as the Rumbling Kern. Eventually it arrives at the 40 metres high basaltic cliff at Cullernose point where the Whin Sill runs into the sea.

Howick had a thriving mineral quarry at Littlemill just to the west of the village. The church was rebuilt in 1746 and refashioned in Norman style in 1849. Just before the Howick Burn reaches the sea are the remains of an even older settlement thought to be an Iron Age earthwork some 60 metres across.

Haltwhistle Burn

Northumberland

RIVERS AND BRIDGES

Northumberland is often described as the land between the Tyne and the Tweed. In fact this is quite untrue as a large section of the county is found to the south of the Tyne and another smaller but still sizeable part is situated north of the Tweed.

The rivers of Northumberland have always acted as highways but it is only the Tweed which serves a function as a national boundary. The small village of Horncliffe perched on a red cliff above the river marks the spot where it ceases to be tidal, below it stands the Union Chain Bridge one of the oldest suspension bridges in the country.

Although the Tweed rises far to the west in Scotland two of her tributaries have played their part in Northumberland's history. The Glen flows along the northern slopes of the Cheviots and at Yeavering stood Ad Gefrin the palace of the Anglo-Saxon kings of Northumbria. Not only is it renowned for its secular importance during the reign of King Edwin, but it was here that Christianity found a foothold in the north.

Joining the Glen to the west of Doddington, the Breamish has flown down from the high slopes of the Ingram Valley and here both become the Till flowing past Etal Castle before surrendering to the Tweed. Very close to the source of the Breamish is the birthpalce of a river that has influenced the county in a lingusitic manner. What would Alnham, Alnwick and Alnmouth be called if not for the river, even if they are all pronounced differently? The Aln rises in the lower Cheviots but originally joined the sea at Amble where you can still see the original mouth where it once joined the Coquet.

The most romantic of Northumberland's rivers the Coquet, has a charm of its own in its upper reaches where it passes Alwinton, Holystone and Hepple widening out to give superb views of its valley before entering Rothbury. Its lower reaches are marked by the wooded ravines at Brinkburn and Warkworth until finally it widens out to enter the sea past the coal staithes at Amble.

Not all of our rivers have evidence of an industrial past at their mouth. The Wansbeck spills gently into the sea with only a few cobles to keep it company, giving the same sedate air that one encounters at Kirkwelpington, Morpeth and Mitford.

The Blyth too has a unique factor as it is arguably the shortest of our rivers rising just above Kirkheaton. Flowing past Bedlington, where the iron works produced the milestones for the Great North Road and the first malleable rails for the trains of the world to run on, the Blyth nudges the Cambois staithes until finally surrendering to the sea where the great wind turbines stand on the pier.

If the Blyth is the shortest of the county's main rivers then the Tyne must be the longest by virtue of its tributaries. Rising only just inside the boundary with Scotland, the North Tyne today forms Keilder Water before being joined by the Rede and eventually passing under the bridge at Chollerford, as it did when the bridge carried the Roman Wall over its waters, before joining the South Tyne just west of Acomb.

In contrast to our other rivers the South Tyne rises not in Northumberland but on the bleak North Pennine moors of Cumbria. Its two main tributaries however; the East and West Allen manage to spring forth from the rock inside the county boundaries but only just.

The rivers of Northumberland have played their part in the county's history. Some have given access to the deeper countryside to the longships of the Norsemen whilst others have been panned for gold and silver. Today they still play an active part forcing the salmon and sea trout to run the gauntlet of rod and line before they reach their spawning grounds. From the early days when Celtic missionaries baptised the Saxon converts in their waters the rivers have acted out their role in the tapestry of Northumberland's history, There is no doubt they will continue to do so.

Opposite: Quarrybeck near Brampton

BERWICK BRIDGES

Designed by Robert Stephenson work on building the lofty arches of the Royal Border Bridge began in 1847, it took three years to complete and employed two thousand men in its construction.

Standing 42 metres above the river it is hard to miss. Queen Victoria and Prince Albert opened the bridge on August 29th, 1850 and linked to its construction the engineers demolished parts of the castle, so today the railway station is actually on the site of the Great Hall. There is a large sign on the steps leading to the platform commemorating the fact that here the crown of Scotland was granted to John Balliol rather than Robert the Bruce.

Flowing sedately beneath the town walls the Tweed continues to contribute immensely to the life of Berwick and its sister communities of Tweedmouth and Spittal.

Crossing the river and linking the two banks with four large arches the Royal Tweed Bridge was entirely built out of concrete in 1928 and was opened by Edward VIII when still Prince of Wales.

The oldest of the three bridges is Berwick Bridge (also known as The Old Bridge.) Work on building this bridge began in 1610. It is built of red sandstone at the cost £15,000. The fifteen arches of this bridge are of different spans, from 7.5 metres to 22.5 metres. The second arch on the Berwick side of the bridge is the highest, this was to allow sailing ships to pass under. The construction of this bridge was

The Berwick Bridges. Opposite: The Royal Border Bridge, Berwick upon Tweed

ordered and paid for by James I of England, VIth of Scotland.

The Old Bridge has played a part too in the development of art in this country as it was one of the favourite places of the artist L.S.Lowry. In fact one of his most famous paintings portrays the east end of the bridge with the steep hill leading up to the town. However, there were also other methods of crossing the Tweed for those who preferred not

to use the bridges. Up until the 1950's a little steam ferryboat called the 'Border Chief' ran from Berwick to Spittal with a frequency of every fifteen minutes in the summer. It is probably a racing certainty that Lowry was amongst the passengers as he loved boats of all kinds but he also loved Berwick. When he was staying in Sunderland he would often insist on being driven to Berwick for the day.

THE UNION SUSPENSION BRIDGE

Until the Bridge at Norham was built in the late nineteenth century the Union Chain Bridge at Loan End was the only dry crossing point for traffic across the Tweed between Berwick and Coldstream.

The bridge is the earliest surviving example of a suspension bridge in England and was designed by Captain Samuel Brown, in consultation with the Scottish engineer John Rennie being finally completed in 1820.

For five years the Union bridge had the longest span of any vehicle-carrying wrought iron suspension bridge in the world, some 133.2m. The bridge was also relatively cheap to build, £7,700 compared with around £20,000 for a masonry bridge.

It is technically important in engineering history in that Brown was the inventor of the wrought-iron link which he had patented in 1817.

The bridge used bars in place of the usual cables, these bars are no more than 25 millimetres thick, which from a distance makes them almost invisible. The foundation stone was laid on 2nd August 1819 and it opened on 26th July 1820 just as Telford was starting on the Menai Bridge over the Straits of Anglesey.

The toll keeper's cottage at the foot of the English cliff was demolished in 1955 and a small forecourt was built on the cottage's foundations.

Beside the bridge is The Chain Bridge Honey Farm which makes an enormous contribution to the flora and fauna of Northumberland with over 1600 hives being scattered around the local area and the borders.

Just downstream is the village of Horncliffe, where both Charles I and Oliver Cromwell camped with their armies as the ford here was one of the lowest across the Tweed. The village is the last navigable point up the river and the furthest distance that the high spring tides reach from Berwick.

The Union Suspension Bridge, Berwick upon Tweed

THE WHITE WALL
BERWICK UPON TWEED

To imagine the power and importance of Berwick Castle you only have to look at the White Wall which hugs the slopes leading down to the river. The wall is known locally as 'Breakneck Stairs' and looks much as it did when it was first built between 1297 and 1298.

First mentioned in 1160, but rebuilt by Edward I when he captured it in 1296, the castle changed hands many times in the border wars. However it was not only the Scots who destroyed the castle as King John laid it to waste in 1216 in a show of strength against those northern English lords, who had declared allegiance to the Scottish king.

That punishment in this period was cruel is to say the least an understatement, for example in 1306 the Countess of Buchan was suspended in a cage for four years for her part in the coronation of Robert the Bruce.

Robert the Bruce finally recaptured the castle in 1318 and built a new wall between the castle and the town, as well as strengthening the main castle gate.

From the early 1600s the castle was abandoned and its stone used for building materials in the town. In the nineteenth century further damage was caused when stone was taken for the Royal Border Bridge and the Great Hall finally levelled for the railway station itself.

The White Wall leads down to the Water Tower, from which originally, a strong chain or boom crossed to the south bank of the Tweed to prevent the passage of hostile craft travelling further up the river.

An idea of the strength of the White Wall can be obtained by walking through the archway that allows the riverside footpath to continue along the banks. Here the full thickness of the wall can seen and the strategic value of the Water Tower becomes obvious when standing on its proud battlements.

The White Wall, Berwick upon Tweed

ALNWICK
THE RIVER ALN

The walls of Alnwick no longer circle the town but it is possible to follow their route even today. In fact the side of Bondgate still shows the scar where the walls butted up to it. The only other gate still standing is Pottergate rebuilt in the eighteenth century at the western end of the town.

The two church towers of St Michael, rebuilt in 1470 and again in 1781 and then again in 1863, and St Paul built in 1846 stand out against the roof tops. The two churches still figure in Alnwick's life when teams from the two parishes play the annual Shrove Tuesday football match in the pastures below the castle. Originally the goals were the two bridges that cross the Aln but now two 1.8 metres high 'hales' are specially built for the occasion.

The Aln has also given a name to another entrance to the town, that of Walkergate just below the castle. Here each day in medieval times the 'walkers' would pass out of the town to the river to walk on the fleeces and hides to soften them up for preparation to be worked on in the town workshops.

Memories of the past abound within the old town not only with its narrow alleyways that climb southwards out of the town but in buildings such as the pinfold where stray animals were kept overnight until the morning when the owners could retrieve them.

Alnwick

Situated on the Great North Road Alnwick had its fair share of coaching Inns and one of them, the White Swan, has memories of a later grander age. Within its walls is the complete 2nd class dining room of the S.S. Olympic, the sister ship of the Titanic, removed and transported here when the ship was broken up on the Tyne.

The town has also had an influence on many other rivers across the globe as it was from here that Hardy fishing rods were sent out to the officers of the Victorian Army stationed across the Empire.

MEETING OF
THE WATERS

Known as the 'Meeting of the Waters' the confluence of the North and South Tyne rivers occurs just west of Acomb. The South Tyne has its beginnings high on the North Pennine Moors, flowing past Alston before entering Northumberland below the Roman fort of Whitley Castle.

The river flows on past Lambley and Featherstone Castle. The name is said to have come from the Fueder stones, two standing stones on the nearby hill where in feudal times the locals would gather.

Leaving the hills behind the South Tyne flows onwards past Bellister Castle with its celebrated ghost, The Grey Man, where sometimes the hounds that killed him can be said to be heard baying in the woods.

Flowing past Haltwhistle the river continues until just past Bardon Mill where it joins the River Allen. Continuing along to Haydon Bridge it finally meets the North Tyne just to the west of Hexham at Acomb.

Because of the march of progress the North Tyne now effectively starts from Kielder Water flowing southwards past Bellingham and the sparse mound that is the remains of Tarset Castle.

At Redesmouth the Rede joins the North Tyne after flowing through Redesdale, one of the most well used of the Border raiding routes, and on past

Meeting of the Waters, North and South Tyne

Chipchase and Haughton castles.

Finally, the last bridge to pass under is reached at Chollerford, the latest crossing in a line since the Romans built their bridge here to take Hadrian's Wall on to its eastern terminus.

In a short distance further on the two Tynes meet and form the River that eventually flows through Newcastle and empties into the sea.

The Oakwood Stone, found at the edge of a field in Acomb in the 1970s, and now located in the parish church at St. John Lee, is one of the of the most southerly of the cup and ring marked stones found in Northumberland. It is thought it was probably used as a capstone to cover an ancient stone burial chamber.

CHOLLERFORD

Crossing the North Tyne the one hundred metre long, lofty, five arched Chollerford Bridge was built in 1775, four years after all but one of the Tyne bridges had been swept away by the Great Flood on the sixteenth and seventeenth of November 1771.

From the bridge one can see Chesters Fort, one of the most important cavalry forts on the Wall. Over the course of time the Romans built two bridges here, the first of which was constructed about A.D. 124 during the original building of the Wall.

This bridge was replaced by a much larger one in the early third century consisting of four stone arches supported by three river piers and had an overall length of some 57.5 metres and most of the remaining stonework that can be seen today is from this bridge.

Since the Roman occupation the North Tyne has altered its course and cut into the western bank beneath the fort, the best remains are seen on the east bank where the impressive abutment forms some of the finest remaining masonry structures on the Wall. The fact that it has survived so well is probably due to the skills and workmanship of the stonemasons.

Just to the east is the pleasant village of Humshaugh where there was once a rope-and-pulley ferry which crossed the North Tyne from Barrasford. In 1908 the world's first scout camp was held in Humshaugh for those scouts who had taken their

The Bridge at Chollerford

promise and belonged to scout troops throughout Great Britain.

A fascinating story in the history of Humshaugh is the part played by the old paper mill in the Napoleonic Wars. In 1793, five years after the mill had been set up, the government developed a scheme to devalue the French currency. A number of paper mills in remote parts of the country, including that at Humshaugh, were commissioned to make paper to be used in the printing of bank notes. These notes were sent to Belgium with the British Army under the command of the Duke of York.

LINHOPE SPOUT

inhope Spout is to be found after a short walk in the Cheviot Moors, high in the Breamish valley. Here the water from the Linhope Burn cascades over 15 metres down into a rocky pool below.

For a county that has all the perfect ingredients for waterfalls, fast flowing streams and high hills, Northumberland doesn't have that many. In fact there are quite a few scattered around the county but most are hidden in deep valleys or densely wooded areas that make them difficult to get to.

The local word for a waterfall is 'Linn' although it originally meant a pool as at Roughting Linn. Incidentally there are two Roughting Linn waterfalls in Northumberland, the more famous with its cup and ring mark rocks is to be found near Kimmerston and the second on the Coalhouse burn just to the east of Chatton.

To the west of the county just outside Bellingham is an enjoyable walk up Hareshaw Burn through deciduous woodland with stone steps, over wooden bridges, criss-crossing the burn before reaching Hareshaw Linn where the water spills over the huge red rock and falls some thirty feet into the chasm below.

One of the places where there is a positive parade of waterfalls is in the steep ravine that leads up the Hen Hole at the end of the College Valley. Bubbling down from the great depression that was the birthplace of the glacier which carved out the valley, the stream that will eventually become the College Burn, tumbles over no less than twelve waterfalls. These waterfalls in the Hen Hole may not be as grandiose as Linhope Spout but they give a wonderful sense of nature to the viewer.

Then there are those waterfalls in the county that suddenly appear as you turn a corner, making the journey that little bit more enjoyable. Swin Hope on the Alnwick road above Edlingham Castle is a good example.

Linhope Spout

HALTWHISTLE

Ask anyone what town is the geographical centre of Britain and it's a fair bet that the "The junction of streams by the hill" will not spring to their lips. However Haltwhistle claims to be just that and with its twelfth century Church of the Holy Cross and a Pele Tower, now the Centre of Britain Hotel, it has several claims to fame.

The town is on the north side of the South Tyne river, which is crossed by an iron bridge of three arches, erected in 1875.

There has been a recognised market at Haltwhistle since King John licensed it in the year 1207, but it was the Border Reivers that have given the town its turbulent past as it lies in the centre of the Middle March, the most active of the reiving districts.

Just like other areas of Northumberland all through this terrible, lawless time the buildings of Haltwhistle were heavily fortified and remains of these can be seen today.

In fact the town boasts more defensible houses than any other in England. There are a cluster of defensible buildings on the Main Street, including five bastle houses and one pele tower.

The thirteenth century church is the oldest building in the town, with superb stained glass windows by William Morris. Strangely the church has no tower but it does have a sixth century old water stoup and a tomb of a crusader, Thomas de Blenkinsopp who died in 1388.

Haltwhistle

The arrival of the railway to the town in the 1840's opened up Haltwhistle as a mining and quarrying centre. In recent times it has developed more as a service centre for the tourism industry, in particular, for visitors to Hadrian's Wall.

The next crossing of the Tyne, apart form the railway line, is at Haydon Bridge. The original bridge was often chained and barred against reiver attacks. Not more than a mile south of the bridge is Threepwood Hall, birthplace of John Tweddell, classical scholar and archaeologist who died in Athens in 1799. The Hall had to be rebuilt after the great Tyne flood of 1773 and the three arches on the south side were replaced in the early years of the nineteenth century.

CORBRIDGE

The first bridge across the Tyne at Corbridge was built in the thirteenth century but was replaced by the present structure in 1674 which is 147 metres long and has seven wide arches.

It was obviously well built, as it was the only one on the Tyne to withstand the great flood of 1771 when it was said the water was so high that people could lean over the parapet and wash their hands.

The village was founded on its present site in Saxon times and stones from the nearby Roman site were used to construct many of its buildings, such as St Andrews Church, one of the oldest in Northumberland.

The church has a Saxon tower, dating from the eighth century and the main body is a mixture of Gothic and Saxon. The entrance however is Norman, while the large tower arch was apparently taken in its present state exactly as we see it from the Roman camp. The church also has a lych gate constructed in memory of the soldiers killed in the First World War.

Corbridge was already a borough when Henry II came to the throne in 1154 and in 1201 King John granted Corbridge the status of a royal borough.

Corbridge still has two strong towers, the first is Low Hall, a three storey pele built by the Baxter family in the fifteenth century, the nucleus of the building is a medieval tower, three stories high, yet it retains many of its original features including a

The bridge at Corbridge

vaulted ground floor. The second is the famous Vicar's Pele built in the fourteenth century on the south side of the churchyard

The street pattern today remains much as it did in medieval times and houses a range of innovative and interesting shops, pubs and coffee shops.

The town suffered severely during the Border unrest, not only from the reivers from upper Tynedale and Redesdale but also from the Scots. King David occupied the town in 1138 and Robert the Bruce burned it in 1312.

To the south west of the town centre is Dilston Hall, which replaced the earlier Dilston mansions that had been home to the Divelston family and the Earls of Derwentwater.

In 1936, the hall was used during the filming of 'The Minstrel' which starred Douglas Fairbanks Jnr. In the 1950's and 1960's Dilston Hall was used as a Maternity Hospital. It has also seen use by MENCAP as a college.

Haydon Bridge

Northumberland

Churches and Christian Heritage

CHURCHES AND CHRISTIAN HERITAGE

To say that Northumberland is the birthplace of Christianity in these islands is open to debate, and most scholars would undoubtedly put us firmly in our place were we to attempt to do so. However it is a safe bet to argue that the influence of the county on the development of Christianity is immense, and possibly more so than any other.

St Aidan, St Cuthbert, St Wilfrid, and numerous others still have a place in Northumberland hearts, a phenomenon perhaps not so common in other areas of the country. The influence too of the early saints is immeasurable. St Hilda was a follower of Aidan and as Abbess of Whitby presided over the Great Synod where the Roman form of Christianity was adopted over the Celtic model.

Today eider ducks are still known locally as Cuddy Ducks, reminding us of St Cuthbert's time on the Farne Islands, when he was said to feed them by hand. Later on the Normans built their Priory on Lindisfarne in dedication to him.

Christianity has not been the only religion to be followed here as is shown by the Temple of Mithras near Chesters where Roman soldiers once prayed, earlier still the stone circles that stand as distant in time from the Romans as they are to us may well have been used for the same purpose.

Many places with religious significance can be found scattered around the county from Holystone Well to the small church at Kirknewton where an ancient sculpture shows the three kings bearing gifts but also wearing kilts.

Throughout the border troubles churches and abbeys were a favourite target and to protect themselves and their flock the vicars of Corbridge, Embleton and Elsdon constructed huge pele towers. Not to be outdone the monks at Holy island had defences built into the priory fabric, where you can still see the arrow loops and remains of the barbican and perimeter wall.

During the reformation Northumberland's monastic houses suffered as much as those in the rest of the country, whilst both Catholics and Protestants felt the wrath of government under the reigns of Mary and Elizabeth. Most notable of these was Thomas Percy who was involved in the revolt during Elizabeth's reign to restore the old faith and lost his head accordingly.

As the great abbeys of Hexham, Lindisfarne, Brinkburn and Alnwick all suffered at the hands of the commissioner some of the smaller churches remained untouched, leaving us gems such as Old Bewick Chapel, almost Byzantine in its appearance, and the marvellous alabaster tombs of Sir Ralph and Lady Elizabeth Grey at Chillingham.

Sometimes the monastic land granted to Tudor dignitaries ensured the survival of ancient religious sites. This is the case at low Chibburn where the preceptory of the Knights of St John, built in 1313, was turned in to a mansion house

As time progresses other religious forces began to play their part and it is not that difficult to imagine the lead mining workers in the River at Allendale downing tools to hear John Wesley speak. The Methodists, Congregationalists, Presbyterian and other denominations have left their mark too with chapels and churches scattered around the county with particular fine examples found in places such as Widdrington and Belford.

The power of religion was greater than that of the monarch, indeed districts of the county were still officially part of The Prince Bishopric of Durham until the nineteenth century.

Opposite: Lindisfarne Priory

ALNMOUTH

"A wicked place," is how John Wesley described Alnmouth when he visited the village in the 1740s. At that time however Alnmouth was a thriving port with ships from all over Europe visiting.

Perched on a tongue of land formed by the North Sea and the River Aln, the village lies some 4fi miles southeast of Alnwick. The estuary we see today is the result of a huge storm that blew up in 1806 resulting in the river creating a new course and cutting off Church Hill from the rest of the village.

The village started to become prosperous around the mid twelfth century and by 1207 was granted a charter for a port and a market. Indeed during the middle ages Alnmouth was recognized as the most important seaport between the Tyne and Tweed serving Alnwick and the surrounding area.

A small amount of shipbuilding took place in the eighteenth century and this period saw the height of the village's prosperity. The main export was grain (many of the large granaries can still be seen as they were converted into houses in later years) whilst imports included slates, timber and guano. This came about as a direct result of the building of the grain road from Hexham direct to Alnmouth as an attempt to avoid paying export taxes on the Tyne.

The storm of 1806 resulted in the harbour becoming too shallow and the port subsequently

Alnmouth

declined, finally the railway killed off the harbour, but brought visitors to enjoy the seaside. So important did this trade become to the village that the station is actually in Hipsburn but called Alnmouth. In 1864 a road was built connecting the village to the station including the Duchess's Bridge which crosses the Aln and has become the main route into Alnmouth today.

In 1778 the American privateer John Paul Jones

bombarded the town but today's visitors are more peaceful, coming to enjoy the beach that is reached by driving across the golf course. In fact Alnmouth Village golf club, is the fourth oldest links course in England.

In the period from about 1897 to 1902 it became fashionable for the well-off to build large detached villas in coastal villages and Alnmouth has the largest selection of any of the coastal villages.

BRANXTON CHURCH AND FLODDEN

The small parish church of Branxton is perched on a hill to the west of the village, just off the A167 to the north of Wooler. The church has a stumpy spire shaped like a pyramid and massive oak altar rails from the seventeenth century. Inside it also has a fine glass set into the west window showing the regimental badges of those villagers who were killed in the First World War.

Nearby on Branxton Moor is a tall Celtic cross of grey granite, here each year a church ceremony takes place to honour those who fought in the Battle of Flodden.

The cross overlooks the battle site, which is virtually unchanged, and is inscribed 'To the Brave of Both Nations'. Each year as part of the Coldstream Common Riding Festival, the Chief rider, the Coldstreamer, lays a wreath on the memorial to the dead of both nations and brings back a sod of earth from the battlefield into the town.

Over 200 riders set off from the town but only the Coldstreamer and his attendants walk up the hill to the memorial escorted by a piper and by two young guardsmen of the Coldstream Guards. The service is both simple and moving with the last post being sounded and a two-minute silence observed.

The Battle of Flodden took place on the 9th September 1513 and was one of the most disastrous and unnecessary battles fought between England and Scotland. Trapped when the English van and

The Battle of Flodden memorial

artillery crossed the Till at Twizel bridge, which still stands on the Cornhill to Berwick Road, the Scots had no option but to come down from their strong position.

English losses were heavy but the dead Scots numbered between five and ten thousand. The entire inventory of the Scottish artillery, all 17 large guns, were captured and it is said that "the slaughter struck every farm and household throughout lowland Scotland. Among the slain were Lords and Lairds, Earls and Abbots, an Archbishop and the body of King James IV himself".

LINDISFARNE PRIORY

There are few places you can step out of the car, breathe in 2000 years of history and take in breathtaking scenery. The Holy Island of Lindisfarne is one of these places and the ruins of its priory have an unforgettable quality.

The priory we see today was founded in Norman Times as a daughter house of the Benedictine Abbey of Durham. Before that however a far older monastery was here, founded by St Aiden in A.D. 635, consisting of Irish monks who followed the Celtic tradition of Christianity as opposed to the Roman.

Little remains of this community as the buildings would have been wattle and daub construction but an interesting exhibition in the village church gives further details as do the fascinating displays in the Museum and Heritage Centres.

The world famous Lindisfarne gospels were created here and the island will be forever associated with St Cuthbert. The priory was sacked by the Vikings in A.D. 793, the first such raid on a monastic house in England, and these continued throughout the following century. So much so, that in A.D. 875 the monks fled from the island with the body of St Cuthbert, eventually arriving at Durham about a century later.

The Norman priory that we see today started off as a small church but by 1200 the standard monastery plan had been established. It is interesting to note that the monks realised they were not immune to the border troubles and the priory has much evidence of this.

The Prior's lodgings have strong defences, a new perimeter wall with a wall walk was constructed and arrow slits can still be seen today in the upper parts of the west gable above the main doorway.

The Anglican Parish Church is the oldest building on the island and reputed to stand on the site of the original monastery founded by Aidan. Indeed parts of the church date back to the seventh century, several hundred years before the appearance of the Priory.

Lindisfarne Priory

ST AIDAN'S STATUE

Carrying the light of the Gospel St Aidan stands on the lawn outside Lindisfarne Priory. Aidan was an Irish monk from the monastery St. Columba had founded on the island of Iona and as a young man befriended Oswald the exiled king of Northumbria whose family had come to live on the island.

In 633 Oswald fought a successful battle and re-established himself as king, choosing Bamburgh as his main defensive fortress and living nearby at the place of Ad Gefrin near Yeavering.

He then invited the monks of Iona to settle on the island and here Aidan established an Irish Celtic Christian monastery of wooden buildings, consisting of a small church and circular dwelling huts.

This monastery was specifically a teaching establishment and thus was restricted to men and boys where the new skills of book learning, reading, writing and learning Latin - the language in which all the books they could obtain were written.

From Lindisfarne, Aidan evangelised much of northern England, founding numerous churches and monasteries. The missionaries, including Aidan himself, trained in Aidan's school went out and worked for the conversion of much of Anglo-Saxon England. It is said that King Oswald, being worried that Aidan would walk like a peasant, gave him a horse. Aidan however gave it away to a beggar saying he wanted to be on the same level as

St Aidan's Statue, Lindisfarne

the people he met to easier discover something of their background and attitudes. Indeed Aidan's work resulted in many notable pillars of the early church including Hilda, Abbess of Whitby, who made such a tremendous contribution to the evolution of Christianity as we know it today.

After 16 years as bishop of the monastery Aidan died at Bamburgh in A.D. 651. The same day that he died a shepherd boy tending his sheep saw a

vision and decided to enter the church. The boys name was Cuthbert and he was to become one of the most important saints in Northumberland's history. Like St Aidan he became Abbot of Lindisfarne and like Aidan his name lives on in schools, roads and public buildings. In St Cuthbert's case he also gave his name to the eider, where to this day it is still referred to locally as a cuddy duck.

LINDISFARNE CAUSEWAY

Twice a day the sea claims back Lindisfarne for its own, denying access to the island by creating exactly that. The causeway has been in existence a long as humans have tried to cross over to the island and has been caused by the tides pushing the sand and silts together as the northern and southern waters meet.

In fact the same route used to cross the Holy Island sands in the time of Aidan and Cuthbert remains the only access to the mainland. The modern causeway was opened in 1954, forming a permanent man-made link with the mainland, and was again extended in 1965.

Further out in the bay the area exposed by the retreating waters is full of valleys, hidden holes and quicksands. To mark out the footway poles were planted from Beal to the island with refuge boxes placed between.

When the road was laid for motor transport and the bridge built it was thought prudent to place a refuge box here as well, yet every year at least one car and often several walkers are trapped by the tide when they have not heeded the crossing times correctly.

However nature marches on and recently deep pools of standing water have collected on the causeway trapped by sand either side of road when the tide has retreated causing a potential hazzard especially at night when they are difficult to see.

Each year the Pilgrimage of the Cross takes place

Pilgrims crossing the sands to Lindisfarne

when local churches combine to take the Christian message of Northumberland back to its birthplace.

There are few finer experiences than sharing the lonely sands with the eider and redshank whilst listening to the lowing of the seals hauled up on the sandbanks to bask in the sun.

The bay is now managed by English Nature and is a Site of Special Scientific Interest.

BRINKBURN PRIORY

If the ruined abbey nestling in woodland on the banks of a river is one of the most idyllic visions of literature then Brinkburn Priory can lay claim to be one of the finest examples around.

Built on one of the most romantic and peaceful spots in Northumberland, Brinkburn nestles on the side of a loop of the River Coquet surrounded by natural woodland. William de Bertram, who owned the Manor of Mitford, founded an Augustinian priory on this site in 1135 during the reign of Henry I.

The early history of Brinkburn is scant but it is thought that the priory was colonised with monks from Pentney Priory in Norfolk and we do know it was certainly never a wealthy house compared to other monastic sites in Northumberland.

It suffered continuous damage throughout the Border Wars, so much so that the priors and canons petitioned Edward II hoping to obtain financial assistance in view of the losses they had incurred. These losses were not restricted to the Scots however, as in 1419 thieves stole chalices and other goods forcing the Bishop of Durham to threaten them with excommunication if they were not returned within twenty days!

The Priory was dissolved in 1536 under the sweeping reign of Henry VIII. It was used as a local church until the late seventeenth century when the roof eventually collapsed and regular services were abandoned and the site was deserted.

Brinkburn Priory

In the 1830's John Dobson mostly rebuilt the manor house lying next door which incorporates the south range of the cloisters. Habitation of the house ceased in the early 1950's but is once again open to visitors and it has fine views of the Coquet from some of it rooms. Some of the parts of the monastic fabric can be clearly seen inside the house.

On its beautiful sloping site beside the river, the priory is one of the county's best-kept secrets, being almost swamped by the densely wooded valley. With the excellent restoration work being carried out by English Heritage the priory has now become a venue for concerts and events.

Hexham Abbey

HEXHAM ABBEY

The dissolution in Northumberland meant most of our monastic houses fell into ruin and still remain that way today, Lindisfarne and Tynemouth being the classic examples, some even vanished off the face of the countryside all together.

Hexham Abbey however stands magnificently above the roof tops of the town and entering the church through the original south transept many relics of the old abbey can still be seen.

Indeed an impressive feature of the monastic church is the monks' night stair. Well trodden, some of the steps bear scars from the Scots invasion of 1296 when molten lead dripped onto them from the burning roof.

The first monastic settlement was set up here in 674 by a community of Benedictines and soon gained a reputation for scholarship, music and sculpture. Hexham is famous for the amazing Saxon crypt beneath the nave, discovered only by accident in 1725, the barrel-vaulted chamber is an evocative reminder of early days of Christianity. Most of the stone used for the construction of this crypt shows Roman decoration and inscriptions, and may possibly have come from the nearby fort at Corbridge.

The Abbey was sacked by a Danish army in 875 and lay in some state of disrepair until in 1113 a group of Augustinian Canons established a community here.

Very little remains of the monastic quarters but the fourteenth century lavatorium on the exterior face of the south wall is one of the finest remaining in the country.

Hexham has many other buildings of interest, not least the Moot Hall, but one of its most graceful is the road bridge leading into the town. This nine arched bridge was built between 1785 and 1788 by Robert Mylne, who also designed Blackfriars Bridge in London.

The interior of Hexham Abbey

LADY'S WELL HOLYSTONE

Lady's Well, Holystone

Close to the spot where the Roman road to High Rochester crosses the Coquet is a place of sacred legend, where missionaries preached the Gospel and where later a community of nuns built a priory near to a sacred spring.

Lady's Well at Holystone has been known as St Ninian's Well and the Well of St Paulinus. Holystone is an important site in the early Christian history of Northumberland, as St. Mungo's Well on the south side of the village is reputed to be one of St. Kentigern's places of preaching and baptism.

In 1780 the pool was given a rim of masonry and in the middle a tall cross was raised in the centre. The inscription on the cross reads 'In this place Paulinus the bishop baptised 3,000 Northumbrians Easter 627'. This claim is rather doubtful as the Bishop was in York at that time so although the date may be inaccurate the story could well be true.

At one end of the pool stands a statue of St Paulinus brought from Alnwick and at the other end stands an altar called the Holy Stone.

Only the small village church of St. Mary remains as part of the original nunnery and even this was largely rebuilt in 1848-9. The priory was founded by Robert de Umfraville, to whom the Conqueror gave Redesdale. In 1291 there were 27 nuns recorded as living here with 4 lay brothers, 3 chaplains and a master. St. Mary the Virgin Church was rebuilt in the middle of the nineteenth century though parts

of the lower walls are probably Norman.

Above the village of Holystone near an ancient fort is Rob Roy's cave, one of the traditional hiding places of the well known outlaw. Not far away in the dark mass of Harbottle Wood plantation is the waterfall of Dove Crag, which sends its water down the Dove Crag Burn to tumble in to the Coquet below.

Nearby in the grounds of Holystone Manor is Woodhouse Bastle built around 1602, recently

re-roofed it is a rather superior bastle house as it has the unusual refinement of an indoor staircase. On the opposite bank of the Coquet the remains of another bastle house can be seen at Sharperton.

Poppies near Corbridge

Church of All Saints Rothbury. Largely rebuilt around 1850, the Church of All Saints still has its original thirteenth century transepts.
Originally an early English monastery, the church is famous for the remains of a fine Saxon cross (A.D. 800) which still graces its interior.

Northumberland

NORTHUMBERLAND'S GLORIOUS COAST

NORTHUMBERLAND'S GLORIOUS COAST

The Northumberland Coast is forever changing due to factors such as the weather and economic change and it is equally true to say that the coastline has influenced the land itself. Many of us do not realise that the coastline is nationally important in terms of the long stretches of sand-dunes that separate the land form the sea. In geological time however these sands are constantly moving, being shaped by the wind and tides. The classic examples of this are Alnmouth where, after the great storm of 1806, the Aln broke through the dunes cutting off the village from the church and Bamburgh where the sea lapped up over the sands to the base of the cliff.

The port at Alnmouth helped develop communications inland when, in the eighteenth century, the Corn Road from Hexham to Alnmouth was built to avoid the export taxes on grain out of Newcastle and is still used today with many of its original milestones still in situ.

As well as corn Northumberland's ports exported many other commodities and these included lime from Holy Island, coal from Amble, Blyth and Cambois, bottles and salt from Seaton Sluice and shoes from Berwick but the industry most associated with the coast is fishing. For a brief period in time the herring was king on our coastline and the sea helped develop two of the finest wooden built boats ever built. On the Northumberland coastline there are far more suitable beaches than safe ports, so the coble was developed to operate from the shore rather than from harbours. Its origins are said to lie in the Norse longboat and it's not difficult to see why.

The larger vessels were known as keelboats. They stemmed from the Scottish types such as the Fifies which were built on the more conventional keel; a feature the coble does not possess. These boats were larger than the cobles and ranged further in search of their catches.

The Coble & Keelboat Society still work cobles in the traditional manner under sail and they are still being built today. The size of the keel boats to the coble can be graphically demonstrated by the boat huts on Holy Island, all that is left of the keelboats that once made up the island's herring fleet.

Others too reap the harvest from the sea whether they be porpoises close in at Amble taking the crustaceans off the rocks, puffins landing on the Farnes with a bill full of sand eels or seals waiting patiently at the mouth of the rivers for the salmon to return.

Although still commercially important these days the coast has far more of a recreational use. The country park at Druridge Bay offers various activities and birdwatchers are spoiled for choice all along the shore. Lindisfarne Bay is the wintering ground of the pale-bellied Brent Geese and home to a commercial oyster operation, whilst at Lynemouth lug worms are exported all over the world to fish farms and anglers alike.

The wide open beaches support vast number of bathers in the summer months but the sea is unpredictable and unforgiving, and during most months the lifeboats are called out to places such as the causeway at Holy Island or to help a vessel in distress further out to sea.

The link with the RNLI and Northumberland will be forever epitomised in Grace Darling but there is a modern connection in that all of the RNLI's boats that need attention are repaired and renovated at Amble in the local shipyard.

It is this recreational use of the coastline that has continued for over a century, some of it was captured by L.S. Lowry and the information board on Spittal beach is sited on the exact spot the artist painted it.

What then of the future of the Northumberland coastline? Already it is being used in a way no one could have imagined just a few years ago. The wind turbines at Blyth allow us to source power for our ever growing energy needs and this aspect of the coastline's character will continue to develop with schemes for wave energy systems being considered.

Opposite: Budle Bay near Bamburgh

AMBLE

Officially known as Warkworth Harbour, Amble at the mouth of the Coquet was referred to as the 'Friendliest Port' by the many sailors who visited here. Unlike other Northumberland ports Amble's prosperity did not come from fishing.

The town developed into a thriving port during the eighteenth century when the main activity was the shipping of locally produced coal, as is evident by the long coal staithes that still stand in the harbour waters.

Amble was originally settled by the Romans, possibly around Gloster Hill, as this is where a ploughman in the nineteenth century turned up pieces of a Roman altar.

The name of Amble is thought to have come from Anna's Bill or Annabelle meaning a promontory and just off shore of the harbour is the RSPB reserve of Coquet Island.

The sandstone quarried on the island was recommended to The Duke of Northumberland as suitable to make or repair parts of Syon House at Brentford.

Compared to other places the harbour has a large fishing fleet and is still seen as a traditional working port. Boat building has been a traditional feature of the town, and it continues to this day. The larger fishing boats moor right along the harbour wall and land a variety of fish, crabs, lobsters and prawns.

Many parts of the town have been extensively modernised and refurbished. The traditional main street and waterfront areas have been restored and the town now has a town square behind the harbour that contains one of the largest sundials in Europe.

Nowadays the town is geared towards tourism, as is exemplified by the large marina, which is host to around 250 boats and yachts.

Amble Town Square

CRASTER

Perhaps today Craster is best acquainted with the pleasant walk to Dunstanburgh Castle and the excellent kippers that are still produced here by the fourth generation of the Robson family.

At the height of the fishing industry some twenty boats supplied the four yards in the village, with up to 2000 fish a day being split and gutted.

Still very much a fishing village, the harbour was built in 1906 by the Craster family in memory of a brother who died on active service in Tibet.

At the end of the harbour is the base of a stone built tower. This tower originally supported the end of a cable runway that came from the whinstone quarry just inland. Along the cableway stone was brought and stored in the tower before being shot in the boats below that had to come and go on the same tide. The incredibly hard and durable whinstone was shipped off to become the kerbstones of London. The Quarry closed down in 1939 is now run as a nature reserve under the protection of the Northumberland Wildlife Trust.

This whinstone sill continues out into the sea nearby and provides lobsters and crabs with an ideal environment in which to thrive and these shellfish are harvested for most of the year.

Craster Tower stands about a mile from the village, dating from the fifteenth century. This is the home of the Craster family, who have been associated with the area since before the Norman

Craster

Conquest. In medieval times the name was spelt Craucestor or Crawster, hence the crest of the family is a raven or crow, embodying a pun on the name. In a similar way the Greys have a scaling ladder for their crest as the old French word for a ladder is gre, meaning a flight of steps.

It must show how important Dunstanburgh was as there is another pele tower close to Craster at Proctor Steads. Both towers are massively built of the hard whinstone and it is possible that the Proctor Tower was used as a signalling or outpost station of the castle. However in places the masonry appears to predate it.

BEADNELL

With the huge eighteenth century lime kilns dominating its small harbour Beadnell has always had an attractive look about it. The lime kilns became redundant when the fishing industry became so important to the village.

In the summer up to 60 local fishermen worked the keel boats operating out of the harbour often accompanied by boats from Cornwall and Scotland. Three herring yards in the village packed the fish into barrels to be sent off to the Baltic.

These days, despite being one of the most popular holiday beaches, fishermen still work out of the harbour, unique in the fact that it is the only one on the entire east coast of Britain that has to be entered by approaching it from the west.

The handful of surviving coble fishermen feared that the harbour was doomed to be closed when fierce storms breached its outer south wall during the winter of 1997 leaving a massive hole in the structure. Typical of a small Northumberland community the villagers got together and with a supreme effort raised funds for the wall to be repaired with the work being completed in mid 2000.

To the east of the harbour on Ebbs Neuk are the remains of a thirteenth century chapel and buildings. In the late 1700's the huge sweep of Beadnell Bay was popular for horse racing and at the time the village was also well known as a centre for smuggling.

A belt of trees behind the sand dunes shelters the village of Beadnell. In the centre is a three storied pele tower now part of the Craster Arms and just outside on the main road, sheltered amongst the trees, is one of Britain's last surviving AA telephone boxes.

As with most of the coastal villages many of the houses are now holiday homes or offer bed and breakfast accommodation. Nowadays Beadnell is a sought after holiday location with its popular sweeping beach, caravan and camp sites.

Beadnell Harbour

Beadnell Harbour at sunset

Newbiggin by the Sea

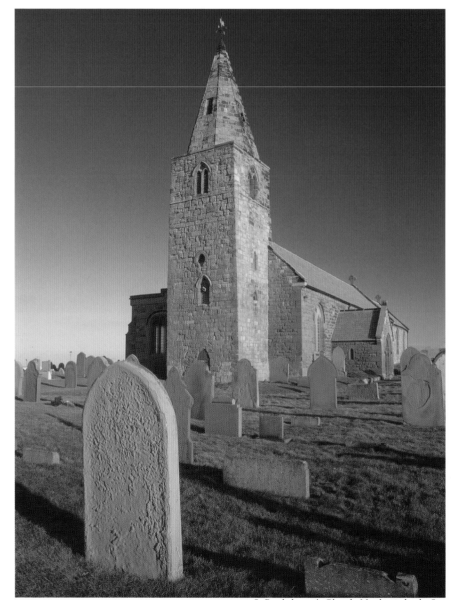

For over 700 years the Church of St Bartholomew has stood on Newbiggin Point and it is thought that a small church occupied this site before 1174, but by the fourteenth century it had become a larger and more important building. During the war mines exploding on the rocks damaged the windows and roof.

Newbiggin is one of the best places to see the traditional Northumbrian fishing coble but it is hard to imagine the busy port it once was. In fact at one time in its history it was a major port for the shipping of grain. It is said that it was third only in importance after London and Hull.

Newbiggin was at the forefront of early telecommunications when in 1868 the first telegraph cable from Scandinavia came ashore at The Point. Floated in on barrels it was laid down in trenches dug by the locals.

The link with the sea is continued by the town's lifeboat as, of all the RNLI's stations scattered around the coast of these islands, Newbiggin's is the oldest operational boathouse in the country.

In 1940 the lifeboat was dragged through the wind and snow by 60 helpers so that it could be launched from the other side of the point when high seas made a launch from the south beach impossible.

Newbiggin also has a literary claim to fame as John Gerard Braine worked in Newbiggin as a librarian. His first novel, 'Room at the Top' was published in 1957 shortly after he left the village.

Just outside Newbiggin by the Sea at Woodhorn are the remains of one of the last working windmills built in Northumberland. Dating from around 1880 it is thought to be on the site of an earlier post or smock mill which burnt down in 1853. The mill probably stopped working in the early 1900 and it seems that the mill also had an external steam engine, to be used when the wind dropped.

St Bartholomew's Church, Newbiggin by the Sea

THE COBLE

This coble at Newbiggin by the Sea typifies the traditional working boat of Northumberland. Still used today and being built today, they are perhaps the least understood aspect of our heritage. The coble's main features are those of a deep forefoot, a flat bottom towards the stern and having no keel.

These characteristics enable the coble to be launched off broad beaches of low gradient into breaking seas, and to be retrieved still facing the breakers, i.e. stern first onto the beach.

Although all of the boats working presently have an engine, it is with sail however that the coble holds its greatest fascination. A working boat carried four sails, a mainsail roughly rectangular and three jibs, large, medium and small (known as 'the Spitfire').

Made of cotton, the sails were tanned in boiling 'Burmese clutch', a tree extract from the Far East which dyed them red. The cotton was dipped in sea water before dyeing in order to fix the colour and stop it running. Under sail the coble is a very fast and lively boat. With the long easy lines it took little to force her through the water and indeed at the turn of the century wealthy Newcastle businessmen adapted them for racing.

In the hands of men who had sailed them all their lives, they came unscathed through the fiercest weather the North Sea could throw at them. A crew of four was the most efficient

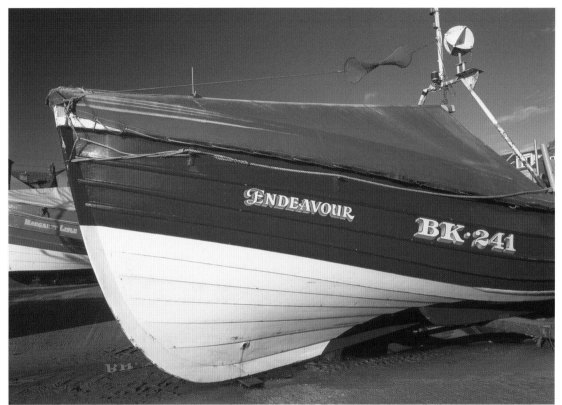

Fishing Coble, Newbiggin by the Sea

working number. Three men would be toiling away whilst the skipper would concentrate on sailing the vessel. All cobles carried two tillers a short one for when working and a long one for sailing.

The Coble and Keelboat Society does a magnificent job in restoring and indeed building cobles as well as sailing them in the traditional manner and amassing an invaluable catalogue and history of the craft. The coble, like other boats, has

evolved over the years. In particular the number of planks visible above the water line has altered with the years and the introduction of the on board motor.

Fortunately as the number of annual sea festivals along the Northumbrian coast increases the coble is becoming known to more and more people. Thus the preservation of what is now recognised as a vital part of Northumberland's heritage is hopefully assured.

DRURIDGE BAY

The long seven mile sweep of Druridge Bay from Hauxley in the North to Cresswell in the South acts not only as a border between the land and the sea but also as one between the rural and industrial sections of the county.

Behind the dunes the Country Park has been created from the opencast mining that went on here. The area is now virtually unrecognisable as a former industrial site with the trees and woodlands planted here gradually maturing.

When the lake was starting to be created in 1974 it broke through into older workings below and its bed had to be relined with clay in the early 1980's. This has been totally successful and the lake is now used for various water sports and in winter provides a refuge for rare bird species such as the smew which comes here from northern latitudes.

In the fields behind the bay stands Low Chibburn preceptory which was built by The Knights of St John in the early fourteenth century to offer shelter and care for the sick and for any pilgrims travelling to Lindisfarne.

The bay is a paradise for bird watchers with its pools and specialist bird watching areas, the dunes are also famous for the spring flowers and the park is very popular throughout the year for the recreational facilities it offers.

The southern end of the bay is bounded by Cresswell with its ancient pele tower and to the north by the village of Hauxley. Just offshore is

Druridge Bay

Coquet Island, now an important RSPB reserve.

At Cresswell, peeping over the park wall of the now vanished Cresswell Hall, is the pele tower. The Cresswells were here in very early times and one of the family is known to have been in possession of the tower in the time of Richard I. It was here that the mysterious White Lady of Cresswell is said to have seen her Danish lover murdered on the beach by her three brothers, a crime which led to her starving herself to death.

Mining and quarrying has played its part in the history of the bay with workings at places such as Chevington and Hauxley. The small village of Low Hauxley seems typical of the small fishing communities that dotted the coast. Now behind it is one of the most successful nature reserves and information centres in the county.

GRACE DARLING'S MONUMENT

Many people make the mistake of thinking that the monument to Grace Darling in Bamburgh churchyard is also her tomb. Actually she is buried with her father and brothers in the nearby family plot.

Grace was born on the 24th November 1815 in Bamburgh. Her father was the keeper of the Farne Islands lighthouses, first on Brownsman and then, at the age of 11, Grace and her family moved to Longstone, when he was appointed the keeper at the newly built Longstone light.

On the morning of September 7, 1838, Grace and her father rescued the crew and passengers of the shipwrecked 'S. S. Forfarshire' which was on its way from Hull to Dundee.

When news of the rescue broke, Grace became a national heroine overnight, being awarded the gold medal of the Humane Society, and receiving £50 from the Treasury. Her portrait was painted many times over, indeed the National Portrait Gallery holds a 60 centimetres high marble bust of her by David Dunbar dated 1838 and many poems were written about her. She died aged just twenty-six, but such was her fame that the memorial was purposefully erected in sight of the sea here in the churchyard.

Close by is a broken column commemorating John Morrel Mckenzie, Professor of Biblical Criticism and Church History at Glasgow, who

Grace Darling's Monument, Bamburgh

when the steamship Pegasus was wrecked on the Farnes in 1843, gathered the passengers around him and prayed aloud as the ship sank. Across the road from the churchyard is the fascinating RNLI museum which is dedicated to Grace's memory.

The village green in Bamburgh is renowned for its trees and at one end of it the village pant still stands facing the castle. In many ways Bamburgh wears its history on its sleeve, take for example the Lord Crewe Arms Hotel named after a Bishop of Durham, thus showing that for most of its history Bamburgh was not part of Northumberland but of Durham.

To the north of the village is the golf course, thought by many to be the most majestic of links courses in the country. The original golf course however was to the south of the castle and traces of it can still be seen. To most people however Bamburgh is linked with its beach, anyone who has walked there will never forget it.

SEAHOUSES

One can't help wondering what the North Sunderland fisherman who, fed up with the long walk from the harbour to the village each day, built the 'sea houses' by the side of the harbour would make of it all today.

In summer Seahouses becomes inundated with people visiting the Farne Islands or diving offshore in its clear waters. However all the development has taken place away from the village above the harbour, as a result it has remained almost as it was in the nineteenth century.

The 'squares' where the lines were baited and nets repaired are still there and in The Neuk you can still see the deep grooves made by the fishermen as they sharpened their knives on the rough sandstone.

At first Seahouses' prosperity came from lime as the massive limekilns on the harbour wall prove. Originally a light railway ran from the local pit to the top of these kilns. Grain was another export and you can still see the granaries on the south of the harbour that have now been turned into apartments.

As with other Northumberland ports the herring was king here and the village has an excellent trail that you can follow with information boards to explain its history to you.

In fact Seahouses folk claim the kipper was invented here when one of the herring store sheds caught fire and the result has graced the world's breakfast tables ever since. Seahouses prominent

Seahouses

feature is its harbour. Built at a cost of £25,000 and opened in June 1889, it was claimed that it could take 300 fishing vessels. To prevent the dynamite used in its construction from exploding and damaging the village a specific store was built on the rocks to the south of the harbour where it still stands today.

A branch railway was constructed to connect with the main east coast line via Chathill. The station and marshalling yards are now the main car park in the village. A line of dark bricks laid in the wall directly opposite the information centre marks out the height of the platform.

UPTURNED BOATS
LINDISFARNE

Looking like a scene out of David Copperfield, the upturned boats on Holy Island's harbour shore are a photographer's delight with their ropes and lobster pots sprinkled around them. A further set of three boats can be found alongside the castle and like their cousins on the beach are used for storage purposes.

They arrived at this their final destination because by about 1875 the herring industry on the island was past its peak and only about sixteen boats were still fishing from here. Whilst the catches on the island dwindled those on the mainland soared.

The final nail in the coffin of the Island's herring boats occurred in 1907 when steam and motor driven boats finally killed off the inshore fishing trade.

The Northumberland keelboats stem from the Scottish types such as the Fifies, Scaffies and Zulus, all of which were built on the more conventional keel; a feature the coble does not possess.

Until the advent of the present day steel hulled trawler, the traditional keelboats of the Northumberland coast were usually larger than the cobles and ranged further in search of their catches.

Directly beneath the upturned boats at the castle are the islands huge lime kilns and directly opposite on the shore of Guile Point can be seen the two

Upturned Boats, Lindisfarne

navigation pillars that ships still use to locate the channel into the harbour.

From the top of the kilns you can still walk on the track of the horse drawn railway to the north shore. This will take you past the Lough, a shallow lake, thought to have been used by the monks for rearing fish, with an overlooking hide where you're quite likely to see a hen harrier dart by or merlins chasing unfortunate pippits in the never ending quest for food.

Amble Marina

Northumberland

HADRIAN'S WALL COUNTRY

HADRIAN'S WALL COUNTRY

Designated a World Heritage Site in 1987, Hadrian's Wall ranks alongside other marvels of the wonders of the world. It is however so easy to imagine Hadrian's Wall as a separate entity in its own right and the most northerly point of Roman occupation in these islands. The wall was built by legionaries at the command of the Emperor Hadrian who visited the frontier in A.D. 122 and wanted to mark the northern boundary of the Empire.

Over six years the legionaries, as well as the highly skilled architects, mason builders, surveyors and carpenters the Roman army numbered amongst its ranks, gradually built up the wall along its 73 mile length to be three metres wide although as it progressed eastwards the width was reduced to 2.5.

At one time the wall was so successful in pacifying the tribes to the south that it was decided to extend the frontier northwards, and it was thus leap frogged by another frontier known as the Antonine Wall that ran from the Clyde to the Forth for a brief period from 140 to 163 in the second century A.D.

This further frontier resulted in Roman occupation across Northumberland as is evident in place names such as Craster and Rochester but the wall still carried out its function as a customs and trade barrier.

To do this, as well as its military function, it had a series of forts and supply depots such as at Vindolanda and Corbridge and a road called the Stanegate running along its length to complete the frontier system.

The Stanegate actually predated the wall as part of the strategy to stop the Brigantes collaborating with the tribes to the North. Also to the south of the wall was the vallum. Flanked by mounds of earth the vallum is a large flat-bottomed ditch that can be easily seen from the road.

Great pains were taken to make this earthwork regular and complete and in places it cuts through the rock. At Heddon on the Wall gaps in the rock forming the sides of the ditch were carefully filled with masonry. It is now thought that the Vallum was a visual boundary into the military controlled area which civilians were only allowed to cross at certain points.

Another ditch was built in front of the wall, purely defensive in nature and can be seen at a number of points, one of the best being at Limestone Corner one mile east of Carrawburgh Fort where the ditch is dug through solid rock.

There is no doubt that the Wall was a sophisticated piece of engineering. At every Roman mile a milecastle garrisoned by up to thirty men was situated and particularly good examples can be seen west of Housesteads and at Windshields, with the latter being built in small masonry as it was probably easier to carry to the site.

Between the milecastles were two turrets essentially acting as signal towers where sentries kept watch. This enabled the supervision of movement of goods, people and livestock crossing the frontier who had passed through the milecastles or forts.

The Romans used the steep slopes of the Whinstone Sill that runs across the country with masterly effect and best preserved and dramatic sections can be seen between Housesteads and Cawfields which is also the highest part of the wall.

In its time the wall was broken by three major disasters marked by burning and destruction and as the Roman Empire declined the wall was abandoned in the late fourth century.

Its legacy lives on however as the stone was robbed over the centuries and used to build other structures in towns and farms. The outlying forts too were gradually robbed of their stone with it being used in some of the county's most magnificent buildings such as Hexham Abbey built with stone from the supply depot at Corbridge.

No journey to Northumberland would be complete without spending some time in Hadrian's Wall Country, visiting the many Roman sites and admiring the magnificent landscape.

Opposite: View from Windshields Crags

BIRDOSWALD FORT

Birdoswald Fort

Although just over the border from Northumberland, Birdsowald is worthy of inclusion in this book because it had an influence on the history of this part of the county.

It is also unique because at no other point along the wall can all the components of the Roman Frontier system be found in such a small area. The curtain walls and three gateways of the fort are excavated and can be clearly seen, the east gateway is thought to be the best preserved along the line of the Wall.

At Birdoswald you can still see the early turf wall built in A.D. 122, over the original fort. The turf wall, stone wall, Harrow's Scar, a milecastle (a short walk along the wall) and the fort itself are all visible reminders of the Roman occupation.

Birdoswald may well be centred around the Roman period, but the fort's history spans over 2,000 years as during the Dark Ages a large hall was built here in the fourth century, possibly by a local chieftain.

In 1211 Walter Beivin held Birdoswold for the payment of one mark. In the medieval period when the border wars were at their height a fortified tower was built here next to the Roman west gate.

The days of the Reivers also saw Birdoswald suffer and a Bastle house was built to protect the Tweddles who lived here. They were raided by the Elliots and the Nixons in 1588 and again in 1590 by the Armstrongs.

The farmhouse built within the walls of the fort dates back to the mid seventeenth century and has been extended on at least two other occasions creating the present façade. In the 1980's the last farmers Mr and Mrs Baxter moved out and the main excavation work began.

As the wall progresses eastwards it passes places with names that resonate the history of the Borders such as Burnt Walls and Thirwall Castle. The de Thirwalls were a warlike family, one of whom lost his life holding a pele on the Forth against William Wallace. John De Thirwall was only 21 at the battle of Falkirk when Wallace's power was finally broken, but by that time he already had five years military experience under his belt.

View over Gilsland

THE WALL

One of the beauties of Hadrian's Wall is the magnificent views it offers along its length. Some of the most impressive views and indeed sections of the wall itself can be seen on the great Whin Sill at Cawfields which is in the care of the National Trust.

The part of the wall between here and Housteads has some of the most dramatic and well-preserved sections. Here the remains of the wall can be stark and inspiring but there is also evidence of the Roman's habit of sticking meticulously to a design. Milecastle 42 adheres exactly to the specified plan for Hadrian's Wall and thus its north gate is sighted above vertical cliffs making passing through it almost impossible.

As the wall travels eastwards it enters a more rolling countryside and here it has merged into the landscape or disappeared altogether with stretches of wall and turrets suddenly appearing again when least expected.

The views the legionaries once enjoyed are now revered by walkers and cyclists, but during the winter months the wall can be an especially fragile environment and great care is needed not to damage it, which can so easily happen.

When finished the wall was coated with a thick coating of weather-proofing lime mortar so it must have appeared as a startling white barrier running across the landscape and amply illustrating the power of Rome. When the Romans left Britain the Wall took on another function, that of a source of building stone that was to last for centuries.

The strangest fact about the Wall however is that it is mostly thought of merely in terms of the stone barrier running along its course that we can see today. However the 'Wall' as we know it was only one small part of an entire system that comprised of ditches, defensive features, signalling towers and outlying forts.

Hadrian's Wall, Milecastle 42

Thirlwall Castle, near Greenhead

VINDOLANDA

Vindolanda is one of the most important and famous sites of Roman Britain. The first permanent turf and timber fort was built here some 40 years before Hadrian's Wall was constructed and formed part of an earlier frontier system called the Stanegate Frontier.

As part of Hadrian's defensive system, around A.D. 120 a new structure was built and attached to the west of this fort. It was a civilian settlement, called a vicus, and is one of the most extensive such sites to be seen in Britain. This fort was enlarged and rebuilt in stone during the early third century A.D. and it is this ground plan that can be seen today.

The name Vinodlanda means white lawns or white fields. It is known that this was the Roman name for the fort because an altar was found during drainage work in 1914. This altar had been set up by the civilians at Vindolanda to the god Vulcan and the name has also been discovered on some of the famous writing tablets.

These writing tablets are a treasure trove of Roman records that give a unique insight into the thoughts and lives of Vindolanda's Roman occupants. The Roman builders spread clay and turf over demolished buildings before starting the later building projects thus sealing the underlying layer preserving everything left beneath it. Objects made of leather, wood, textiles and metal survive in superb condition.

Vindolanda

The Vindolanda Trust carries out outstanding archaeological work as well as educating visitors to the site with a museum, interactive displays and reconstructions of the turf and stone walls.

There is a possibility Vindolanda may well have an imperial claim to fame. During excavations in 1991-93 a superbly fashioned wooden building was uncovered, and it may well be that it was built to accommodate Hadrian and his staff when they stayed here in A.D. 122.

However there is no doubt that Vindolanda is unique amongst the forts that combine to make up the walls entire defensive system. The writing tablets and other artefacts found here make any visit to the site truly memorable.

View east from Cuddy's Crags

VINDOLANDA
ROMAN TEMPLE

On the banks of the Chineley burn, in the museum gardens at Vindolanda, sits a reconstructed Roman temple, dedicated to the nymphs. The temple is part of the open air museum which also includes a Roman milestone, with mock inscription, recording the imminent arrival of the Emperor Hadrian. As well as the Roman temple, with wall paintings in the style of Pompeii at Vindolanda, a Roman shop, Roman house and a Northumbrian croft, all with audio presentations, can also be seen.

However the joy of Vindolanda is the ongoing excavation work carried out by the Vindolanda Trust, which gives visitors the chance to see history in the making.

For example, the excavations have revealed large alder tree trunks which had been bored through with an augur, thus creating a 5 centimetre pipe for the water supply. The individual lengths were connected with rectangular oak slabs - without any use of iron or lead fittings. It is thought that the source of the water was probably the major spring at the western edge of the Vindolanda site.

Some of the most unusual and well preserved objects from the Roman world have been discovered here and in the superb site museum, set in ornamental gardens, the visitor can find Roman boots, shoes, armour, jewellery and coins.

Vindolanda's treasure is the writing tablets that

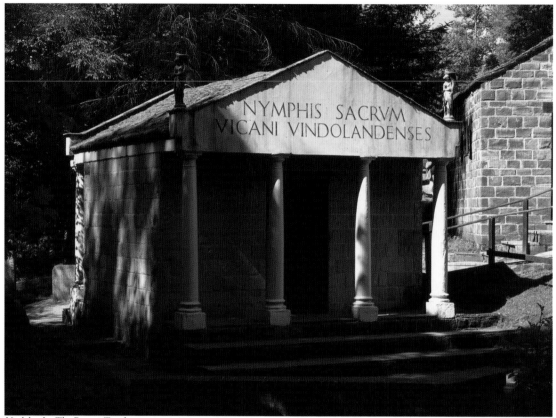

Vindolanda, The Roman Temple

give an amazing insight into the life of its occupants. Made of specially prepared birch and alder wood, the ink writing covers one surface with the address on the opposite side as with a modern letter.

Less than 3 millimetres thick and the size of a postcard the tablets are conserved and photographed, with infra-red photography on site

at Vindolanda.

After initial research they are then sent to The British Museum in London for specialist archival storage. The museum on the site has a comprehensive display about the tablets and the incredibly fascinating information they hold.

View west from Sewingshields Crags

Sycamore Gap near Steel Rigg (above) is renowned as being used as a location for the film industry. Spare a thought though for the Roman soldiers who had to climb up and down the steep banks of the Wall here on sentry duty, their capes wrapped around their faces to try and keep out the cold winter storms.

Despite the passage of centuries the wall continues to possess a feeling of Rome about it. Many of the legionaries who served here left their marks on the wall in the shape of plaques or memorial tablets. At certain times during the year you can see the spectacular of re-enactment groups of the Roman legion (top right), providing a fascinating look into life on the Wall, with full displays at sites including Corbridge and Vindolanda.

There is a magnificent view (right) towards Sewingshields Crags from Housesteads. Sewingshields is one of the best places to view the vallum. Indeed a short distance to the east the road cuts across this monumental earthwork, giving the visitor excellent views of its construction.

Crag Lough from Hot Bank Crags

HOUSESTEADS

Sitting on a spectacular position with commanding views, Housesteads Fort is without doubt the most famous of all the forts built along the wall.

To the Romans Housesteads was known as Vorcovicium, a name of Celtic origin probably meaning 'The place of the effective fighters', it also has the distinction of being the most complete example of a Roman fort to be seen in Britain today. Housesteads had barracks that could accommodate around 800 to a 1000 men and for much of its history Germanic auxiliary soldiers from Tungria garrisoned the fort, although there was possibly some local recruitment.

Unlike other forts on the Wall Housesteads is built on quite a noticeable slope. The Romans were nothing if not a practical people and the granaries, one of the most memorable parts of a visit here, were built on the highest part of the fort to keep the food inside dry.

There was an open area to the west of the granary to allow carts to unload and turn and to the south of the fort a system of terraces was employed to increase the agricultural land available.

After the Romans left Britain Housesteads fell into decay, although human habitation did continue off and on and the fort became a haunt of criminals and cattle rustlers during the time of the Reivers.

Built against one of the guard chambers of the fort's southern gateway, is the bastle house of the

Housesteads Fort

Armstrong brothers. Now only the ground floor remains where the animals were kept whilst the family lived above. Housesteads is now in the care of English Heritage.

Down the slope to the east, in the valley of the Knag Burn, a gateway was placed in the Wall, with doors at both the front and the rear, for customs control under the supervision of the garrison above. This shows that the Wall not only served as a defensive barrier but also as a political one. It also illustrates that at the time of its insertion the Roman's felt strong enough to incorporate what is essentially a weak defensive point into the Wall.

Housesteads Fort

Aerial view of Chesters Roman Fort

CHESTERS ROMAN FORT

Chesters Roman Fort

The fort at Chesters is the most picturesque of all the Roman forts in Northumberland and marks the point where Hadrian's Wall crossed the river North Tyne with the Wall continuing right down to the water's edge.

Chesters was a cavalry fort and as is normal for cavalry forts along its length, it was built either side of the line of the Wall, with three of its major gateways opening out onto the northern side to allow for rapid deployment of the Roman legionaries and cavalrymen.

The fort consisted of the usual rectangular stone outer wall with curved corners, surrounded by a deep outer ditch. The bath house, however, is quite substantial and is one of the more complete examples to be found along the wall.

Also visible are the remains of a Roman stone bridge abutment. The first bridge was built around the time of the original construction of the wall. However this bridge was rebuilt on a far more impressive scale in the early third century A.D. and it is these remains that are visible today.

At the turn of the 1800's the owner of Chesters House and estate covered over the last remains of the fort as part of his parkland landscaping. However in 1832 he was succeeded by his son John Clayton who was fascinated by the remains of the Roman presence in the neighbourhood and went to the trouble of removing his father's work, exposing the fort, excavating, and establishing a small museum for his finds.

As with most of the other Roman forts in the empire Chesters had a civilian settlement outside the walls. In Chester's case it was to the south and southeast heading towards the North Tyne. Here the garrison would have spent their hard earned cash in taverns and shops and possibly kept a family. Chesters individuality is owed to the serenity of the river and the trees that grow around it. It is also intriguing in that you can actually look down on sections of the wall where they have been exposed from underneath the eighteenth century landscaping.

View north from the Military Road near Chollerford

CORBRIDGE ROMAN SITE

It is often forgotten that Hadrian's Wall was not a defensive unit in its own right, but rather it formed part of a system of forts and roads that acted as complete customs barrier and supply chain.

One of the most important of these was at Corbridge just north of the present town. It occupied a strategic position at the point where the Stanegate, the road running parallel with the wall towards Carlisle, met Dere Street the main road into Scotland where it crossed the Tyne.

The history of the fort can be put into four distinct stages with work on it being abandoned around 180 when a northern uprising took place and broke through the wall and caused much destruction in the surrounding area before being brutally put down.

One of the sites of Corbridge is the remains of the fountain house which was the main distribution point for the public water supply. When allied with the aeration tank and aqueduct the structure gives one a remarkable insight into the ingenuity and sophistication of Roman life.

The fort became the main supply depot for the armies building and guarding Hadrian's Wall and the site contains the best example of military granaries in the country which are very impressive with raised floors. Eventually over a period of years the fort developed a prosperous garrison town outside the complex that covered some 11 hectares.

Corbridge Roman Site

Much of the stone was taken away from the fort in later years for building projects, some for Hexham Abbey. Today the site is in the care of English Heritage.

Interestingly enough it is thanks to the builders of the abbey that when they took the stone from Corstopitum, as the Romans knew the fort, they preserved the tombstone of a cavalry regiment's Standard Bearer called Flavones. His unit of cavalry is thought to have been stationed here in the first century and his tombstone is one of the best examples in existence. It shows the 25 year-old riding down an unfortunate warrior and states that he had already served seven years in the regiment.

The Temple of Mithras near Chollerford

HEDDON ON THE WALL

The stretch of broad wall at Heddon-on-the-Wall shows that the eastern section of the wall was built up to a width of ten Roman feet* whereas further west it is only some eight Roman feet but stands on the broad wall foundation.

However, as with most Northumberland villages, there is a lot more history in Heddon-on-the-Wall than first meets the eye. The parish church of Saint Andrew's has been added to over the years, but some of the building dates back to the Saxon period of A.D. 680.

After the foundation of Blanchland Abbey the monks were given land around Heddon by Walter de Bolbec and it was they who became responsible for the church.

In 1796 the local mine owners built a row of cottages for their workmen at the eastern boundary of the parish. As the buildings were being completed French Loyalist clergy refugees, fleeing from the Revolution, arrived in the Tyne and 38 of them settled in the cottages.

The refugees eventually returned to France in 1802 and to show their gratitude they erected a sundial on the front of the row of cottages which today are still known as 'Frenchman's Row'.

Heddon-on-the-Wall also has a connection to the newspaper industry as during the second World War the old workshops at Heddon colliery yard were taken over and used as an emergency

Heddon on the Wall

printing works for what is now the Newcastle Chronicle & Journal.

The 275 metre long section of the wall here gives us a good insight into how the interior core was built. However, just to the south there is also an excellent stretch of the vallum. The solid rock it runs through is covered with moss and grass but every now and then the tool marks made by the

legionaries can be still seen and in a few places where there are gaps in the rock the masonry inserted by the Romans as fill can still be seen.

It is also interesting to note that until the deepening and embanking of the River Tyne, it is said that this was originally the highest point reached by the tidal waters.

* Roman foot is 29.67 centimetres. Roman mile is 1480 metres.

Roman re-enactment, Chesters Fort

Northumberland

INDUSTRY AND TECHNOLOGY

INDUSTRY AND TECHNOLOGY

As long as humans have been in Northumberland they have influenced the landscape with their constant need to advance the quality of their lives by developing industry and technology.

The first recorded evidence of this comes from some 6000 years ago when the hunters and gatherers of the Mesolithic age left the evidence of their flint tools at Newbiggin-by-the-Sea and Budle Bay. Flint arrowheads have been found at Rothbury whilst at Whittingham, Bronze Age swords and spears were discovered looking now almost as they did on the day they were forged.

The Romans mined here and throughout the middle ages both the land and the living rock were worked for profit. Water and wind power reigned in this time with windmills sprouting up but sadly only about a dozen still remain. Watermills survived for much longer and one is still doing so at Heatherslaw near Ford whilst one can only wonder how thriving the mill complexes of Hexham, Felton Park on the Coquet and Waren Mill on Budle Bay must have been.

Remnents of the industrial past litter the county especially with the number of quarries to be seen. Some date from Roman times whilst others from the twentieth century have now been flooded to make recreational parks and nature reserves.

As the centuries passed the Industrial Revolution arrived and the age of steam made the most dramatic mark yet on the landscape. The valley of the East Allen became the centre of the richest lead mines in Europe with its chimneys and flues still visible on the surrounding moors. Blanchland and Langley smelt mills are no more and have gone the way of the enormous airship hangar that once stood at Nelson near Cramlington.

Many other facets of our industrial past have also disappeared or fell into ruin. The paper mills at Fourstones and Haughton Castle, the brick works at Belsay and Capheaton, the salt pans at Hartley, the bottle factory at Seaton Delaval and the clay works at Kirwhelpington all employed many people during their time but now, like the great coal mining industry, little sign remains.

Coal was the major industry in Northumberland. We know it was being mined at Plessey Woods in the thirteenth century, and it resulted in development of ports such as Blyth and Amble and fascinating architecture such as the timber trestle carrying the railway over the Sleek Burn at Choppington. Long rows of terraced houses can still be found both in the towns and in small villages with the prime example being Linton to the west of Ashington which itself was no more than a farm in the early years of the nineteenth century.

Were it not for the coal industry in Northumberland the world would be a very different place. The work carried out by George Stephenson at Killingworth Colliery laid the foundation stone for the railways to open up the world's untamed wildernesses and sow the seeds for universal trade and commerce.

The great soil heaps that dominated the skylines are now landscaped with grass and trees, and many of the wagon ways and railway tracks have been converted into cycle tracks or bridle paths.

Railway tracks criss crossed the county at one time from Alnwick to Cornhill and Hexham to Allendale leaving disused stations such as Glanton, Ilderton and Langley, which have been turned into homes or businesses. A range of smaller branch lines carrying lead, iron and coal also abounded, one of the most used of these lines ran from Seahouses to the main line at Chathill so that fish could be taken the great city markets.

Today industry and technology work hand in hand and still leave their mark upon the landscape. The great fountains at the Alnwick Garden work on a combination of computer and turbine pumps. Our lighthouses are run by the computer chip but perhaps the most impressive are the wind farms that thrust up from the sea off Blyth.

Opposite: Blyth Wind Farm

ALLENDALE TOWN

Although it is referred to as 'Town' this was to distinguish the settlement of Allendale from the surrounding valley of the same name but as the population is only in the hundreds, it is officially regarded as a village. Amongst the devotees of North East author, Catherine Cookson, the valley is known as Mallendale as it was used the setting for her 'Mallen Streak' trilogy.

The lead mining industry was the major employer here at one time and the smelt mill for the valley continued in use up until 1896 and signs of the industry are all around.

In the nineteenth century Allendale became a highly popular tourist destination and to a large extent this is still true especially on the 31st December each year. Allendale Town is world famous for its Tar Barrel Ceremony each New Year's Eve. Thousands of people travel here from far and wide to see the local men, known as 'Guisers', wearing fancy dress, and carrying flaming barrels of tar on their heads.

The procession marks the boundary of the village and ends at midnight in a spectacular bonfire in the Market Place. Folklore suggests it goes back centuries and is connected with pagan celebrations of the winter solstice.

 Other evidence suggests that while the fire might be a longer tradition, the tar barrels themselves are a more recent fixture as it is said that in 1858 some men making their way to the Methodist church

Allendale Town

were annoyed at their tallow candles being blown out by the wind and used a tar barrel to illuminate their music.

The village is surrounded by the high moors covered in heather and rich in wild life with the huge chimneys from the lead mining industry still visible above. The two giant brick flues leading up to them can be easily seen as well.

There has been a settlement here for at least 1000 years. Although there is much debate with Haltwhistle, Allendale regards itself as the geographical centre of Great Britain in having been recorded as such in 1842. This was derived from taking the latitude and longitude readings on the sundial at Saint Cuthbert's Church in the Market Place.

THE ALNWICK GARDEN GRAND CASCADE

Built on listed embankments dating back to the 1850's The Grand Cascade hides the remains of vast underground tunnels which provided hot air for earlier greenhouses. Built of Darney Stone from West Woodburn in Northumberland, the Cascade is split into two apparent sections. Water falls down the first 27 weirs, disappearing into four large bell mouth openings, to reappear at the other side of a walkway in four 'mounds' of water.

Designed to be as environmentally friendly as possible, 250,000 gallons of water are stored underground at any given time, and are filtered and recycled to create spellbinding water displays. Constructed in a series of 30 weirs, 7,260 gallons of water per minute tumble down the Cascade at peak flow. Water is circulated up and down a vertical drop of nearly 30 metres. In the event of heavy rain, overflow water is discharged directly into the nearby River Aln, without fear of contamination.

The water displays within the Cascade are switched on at 10am daily and change sequence every half-hour throughout the day, with four sequences in total. The sequences are largely computer-controlled by state of the art equipment in the pump room below.

During the sequences, three large central jets reach a height of 6 metres, with 40 smaller jets sending water 4.5 metres into the air. 80 side jets

The Grand Cascade, The Alnwick Garden

form parabolas of water to the centre of the Cascade and four jumping jets issue from the four bell mouths, firing streams of water over the walkway into the Grand Basin below. The climax of the display is an eruption of fountains forming a mass of water which, at its peak, reaches a height of 6 metres.

The Grand Cascade offers something missing in so many other large garden water features in that one is able to walk completely around it, and therefore can view the jets and fountains from a variety of angles and heights, thus enhancing the overall enjoyment.

BLYTH

Today Blyth is a modern thriving port handling up to one million tonnes of cargo each year. The history of Blyth as a port dates from the twelfth century and one of the first railways in England was laid here in the seventeenth century from Bebside Colliery with wooden rails and carts pulled by horses. The port reached it peak as a coal shipping port by the early 1960's. The area has always been dominated by heavy industries but with the closure of the shipyard and pits, by the mid 1980's change was inevitable.

Blyth is famous for its 'Lighthouse in the street', which was built in 1788 by Sir Matthew White Ridley who owned Cowpen Colliery and had his own coal staithe at the harbour. When it was built it was only 10 metres from the water but development over the years has resulted it in being now found in the back lane of Bath Terrace.

A feature of Blyth's present importance is the quayside of the outer harbour wall where there is now a row of nine 300kW Windmaster turbines that generate 'green' electricity. Just off shore is a landmark project in the first step of a new power generation industry in Britain.

The offshore wind farm being built is eventually expected to contribute a sizeable amount to the country's renewable energy. At the time of their construction the turbines were the largest erected offshore in the world.

Blyth also has strong sporting connections, it is the home of the Royal Northumberland Yacht Club and Blyth Spartans is one of the most highly regarded and successful non-league football teams.

In St Cuthbert's churchyard is buried William Carr who died in 1825 and weighed 24 stone. He was said to be a very strong man and on one occasion vaulted a five barred gate with an eight stone woman under his arm, and on another occasion he carried a half ton anchor from a ship to the smithy. It is not generally known that the first of all English railways was laid down from Bebside Colliery to the river in the early seventeenth century.

Wind Turbines, Blyth

THE CONSTRUCTION OF HADRIAN'S WALL

Along its length the construction of Hadrian's Wall was not uniform. In fact in places it is decidedly narrower than others and very different materials were used. The wall was built as a customs barrier and above all, to impress and so it needed to be imposing. It required nearly 40,000 tons of stone per Roman mile and also huge quantities of lime to set the ashlar facing.

In places the wall was originally built of turf but later covered over in stone. Also the wall was originally meant to be ten Roman feet* thick but this was reduced to eight in places. Indeed the base of the broad wall was built virtually from Newcastle upon Tyne to the crossing of the North Tyne but the change was made abruptly and the narrow wall was placed on top of the broad wall foundations.

The change of thickness in the wall may well be connected with a change in constructional technique. In the broad wall the facing stones are set in mortar, but the rubble core was usually set in clay as this allows slight movements to take place in the structure and reduces the amount of lime needed.

However, on the steep slopes the wall encountered, the flexibility of clay was not so important. Since mortar was stronger the wall could be made less thick and still be raised to the same height, thus saving using thousands of tons of stone in the construction.

Seven metres in front of the wall, a deep ditch was cut. The material dug out from it was carefully spread out on the northern lip to heighten the slope without giving cover to an approaching enemy.

The ditch was even cut through solid rock, except where cliffs or the sea made it unnecessary. On the crags of the Whin Sill for instance the ditch is missing, but in the nicks between them short lengths of ditch were cut sometimes extending for no more than 30 metres.

* Roman foot is 29.67 centimetres.

Peel Crags, Hadrian's Wall

GEORGE STEPHENSON'S BIRTHPLACE

The most historically important stretch of railway in the world no longer remains but the track of the Wylam wagonway can still be walked upon. Immediately beside the track way is the small cottage in which George Stephenson was born in 1781 and one of his first duties was to ensure his younger brothers and sisters did not get run over by the horse drawn wagons.

This small stone tenement was built around 1760 for mining families, Stephenson's father being the fireman at the Colliery hence their occupation of the cottage. The building is now in the care of The National Trust and the furnishings reflect the year of Stephenson's birth, his whole family living in the one room.

George had little schooling and only learnt to read and write at the age of 19 when he attended night school. At the age of thirty-one he was appointed 'engine wright' at Killingworth Colliery and he began to design his engines. With the wealth he amassed from his inventions Stephenson organised night schools for miners, recreation rooms and schools for miner's children.

In 1812 William Hedley, who was born at Newburn was commissioned by Christopher Blackett, the owner of Wylam Colliery, to produce a steam locomotive. He produced an

George Stephenson's birthplace, Wylam

engine called Puffing Billy named after him, a forerunner to Stephenson's Rocket.

There is one more well known engineer associated with Wylam, Sir Charles Parsons who lived at Holeyn Hall and it was here that he invented the first multi-stage steam turbine.

The wagon-way at Wylam was just one of many that sprang up over the county. Some such as on Holy island are in a good state of repair whilst others are remembered in song. The Plessey Wagonway, built about 1709, is a Blyth song published about 1903 and still heard in folk clubs.

LEAD MINING

The North Pennines were a major source of lead ore, with several centres of mining and processing. In Northumberland the industry was centred around the Allendale area. Originally a farming area, in the eighteenth and nineteenth century the valley rapidly expanded as a lead mining centre with the ore being mined at Allenheads and other locations and then smelted at Allen Mill.

Underground huge flues were built that directed the fumes miles away to chimneys on the fell top. This was to enable the lead, which solidified on the walls of the flues as the fumes cooled, to be scraped off and finally collected. Tall chimneys can still be seen on the top of the fells.

One of the by-products of lead smelting is silver and it is thought that perhaps the name Allendale in Celtic refers to a river containing traces of silver, hence, 'valley of the shining water'.

However lead was not the only mineral mined here. Near the hamlet of Spartylea between Allendale Town and Allanheads, is the St Peter's mine. Originally worked for lead in the late nineteenth century during the first half of the twentieth century the Weardale Lead Company worked it commercially for fluorspar.

The mine is best known for producing some very good quality specimens of bright apple-green fluorite during the 1930's, which are now held by the Natural History Museum. A few years ago a group of collectors and cavers leased the rights to work the mine, using hand tools only, for specimens.

The chimney shown here is from Sikehead near Blanchland and was built for the mine's pumping engine.

Lead mining remains at Sikehead near Blanchland

LONGSTONE LIGHT

Now run by computer but built between 1825 and 1826, The Longstone Lighthouse marks the outermost of the Farne Islands. Four nautical miles from Seahouses harbour it was the home of Grace Darling when she made her famous rescue. The islands represent one of the most dangerous hazards to shipping around the entire British Isles and have claimed numerous victims over the centuries.

Often called Britain's Galapagos Islands, the Farnes form a small group of 16 islands, that increase to 28 at low tide, in two distinct groups. The Outer Farnes or northernmost group are made up of 'Staple', 'Brownsman', 'Big Harcar' and 'Little Harcar', 'North' and 'South Wamses' and 'Longstone' Islands.

The Inner Farnes or southernmost group consist of east and west 'Wide Opens', 'Scarcar' and the 'Inner Farne'.

Now in the care of The National Trust they offer a truly memorable experience for any one visiting them. Today soil erosion is a serious problem on the islands, but it is being dealt with by the splendid scientific work of the Trust. There are no trees on the islands and only a few bushes grow that were planted by the previous lighthouse keepers to shelter their vegetable plots.

It is the birds that are the glory of the islands with tens of thousands of breeding puffins, guillemots, eiders, kittiwakes and terns. Many of the birds are contemptuous of humans and visitors can enjoy close views but a hard hat is recommended! There is also a large colony of seals living around the islands. St Cuthbert died on Inner Farne in 687 and the chapel built in his memory still stands.

For eight months of the year the island's are occupied by National Trust wardens living on Inner Farne and Brownsman.

Longstone Lighthouse

SEATON SLUICE

The modern day village of Seaton Sluice is made up of what were once the two entirely separate villages of Seaton Sluice and Old Hartley. In the thirteenth century Hartley Pans was an important centre for salt production, where seawater was evaporated in huge pans heated by coal fires and the salt shipped to southern ports such as Yarmouth and Norwich for use in herring curing.

However the entrance to the mouth of the Seaton Burn was treacherous and awkward for ships as the incoming tides swept in silt and sand that blocked the narrow entrance, and at low tide the harbour was left high and dry.

In 1660, to solve this problem, Sir Ralph Delaval started the building of a stone pier to create a harbour, Hartley Haven, and 10 years later he received a royal grant to carry out further improvements.

In 1690 Sir Ralph had sluice gates built which closed as the incoming tide filled the harbour and dammed the flow of water in the Seaton Burn. At low tide, after horse drawn ploughs had loosened the deposited mud and silt, the sluice gates were opened and a powerful flood of water flushed the harbour clean. It was because of this inspired engineering solution that the port became known as Seaton Sluice.

Seaton Sluice harbour

As well as salt the harbour exported coal. The Royal Hartley Bottleworks, which once dominated the harbour, was one of the largest of its kind in England. In 1777 production reached a staggering one million seven hundred and forty thousand bottles a year.

During the second World War the tunnels of the factory were used as air raid shelters. Hartley had an American camp just south of the Sluice during the war whilst Seaton Delaval Hall held German and Italian prisoners.

ALNWICK
TENANTRY COLUMN

At the south end of Alnwick stands the Tenantry Column built in 1816. The story goes that the peace after the Napoleonic wars resulted in reduced prices in the market place and meant a cash flow problem for the farmers on the estate who were unable to meet their rents. They commented on this to the Duke who reduced the rents accordingly.

The tenants in their turn, to show how much they appreciated such generosity, built the column, topped by the Percy Lion to express their gratitude to the Duke. This was inscribed: 'To Hugh, Duke of Northumberland, by a grateful and united tenantry.'

The Duke decided that if they could afford such a gesture then they could afford the rents that were promptly raised again. Thus the column is known by its local name the 'Farmers Folly'.

Beneath the column on the main road is the war memorial and amongst the names listed here is that of the ninth Duke who was killed at the age of 27 whilst serving with the Grenadier Guards in the British Expeditionary Force in France in 1940.

Opposite the war memorial is the old railway station and the trains ran from here on a spur line to the main east coast line at Alnmouth. Nowadays it is one of the largest second hand bookshops in the country but still retains many details of the Victorian station inside which have been carefully restored and used in the fabric of the building.

Proceeding eastwards from the column along the road towards Alnmouth the sedate villas built by the well off, who no longer wanted to live inside what they saw as the cramped area of the old town, start to appear. The contrast to the west end of the town could not be greater with trees, large pleasant gardens and gated drives.

The Tenantry Column, Alnwick

Tumbleton Lake, Cragside Gardens near Rothbury

Kielder Castle

Northumberland

Rocks and Landscape

Rocks and Landscape

The oldest rocks in Northumberland date back some 450 million years. Some 50 million years later the great volcanoes finally died and left the Cheviot Hills as a reminder of their existence.

Later on other volcanoes squirted layers of molten rock through the layers of the softer sandstones eventually forming the Whinstone outcrops on which Bamburgh Castle and Hadrian's Wall now stands at its most spectacular points.

Limestones were laid down and like other rocks suffered huge earth movements twisting and breaking them into anticlines and folds that can still be seen in quarries and on the coastal cliffs. Coal and lead were formed and lay waiting in the ground for the mining industries to release them.

The ice ages came and went with the glaciers gouging out deep valleys and depositing rocks and clay from their meltwaters. After they retreated the water levels rose and formed the coastline virtually as we know it today.

There is no doubt that man has influenced the Northumberland landscape. The great forests only survive in remnants and the hedgerows and plantations have forced a rhythm of life on the animals and birds of the county that it would be difficult to change.

Reservoirs and lakes have been created, whole swathes of countryside buried under tarmac and concrete. Abandoned buildings litter the land from the industrial age, slowly crumbling under the very same forces that shaped the land.

But it is maybe just as true to say that the Northumberland landscape has affected those who have lived in it as long as humans have been here. From the earliest times the need for survival and profit forced them to plough in the rich coastal plains or dig on the high slopes.

The rocks were drawn and carved upon as we see in the cup and ring mark stones that are sprinkled across the county and these rocks have resulted in the network of our dry stone walls having their own peculiar Northumberland characteristics.

Sometimes their domestic animals escaped and colonised the hills where now they are seen as the herds of feral goats leaping from crag to crag. Sometimes man enclosed areas trapping animals inside, encapsulating them in time, so hundreds of years later they remain the sole survivors of their breed as with the Chillingham Cattle.

Probably at no other point in the history of the county has it been so well known and used by the human population. At weekends and in the summer months the high hills of the Cheviots and North Pennines play host to walkers and ramblers whilst the coast and the newly constructed country parks provide recreation of a less strenuous type.

Even the remnants of the industries that polluted the land have been utilised, be they the spoil heaps from the coal fields of the southeast that have been replanted with trees and given over to local walks, or the huge smelt mill floors of the lead industry that now attract tourists and give jobs to local people.

In our own time open cast mining has gouged out, and still continues to do so, great scars on the landscape, yet even these will eventually be reclaimed by nature and become a haven of wildlife.

The same can be said of the extensive country parks and gardens created by the great families. The Percys, Armstrongs, Blacketts and others employed men to move massive boulders and thousands of tons of earth to create the vistas that their owners required. Now these same artificially created landscapes bring local employment to places such as Cragside, Alnwick, Belsay and Wallington.

The Northumberland landscape is in a constant state of change, being sculpted by elemental forces and the activities of mankind.

BOLAM LAKE

The area around Bolam is rich in Northumberland's history. The modern day country park surrounds Bolam Lake, an artificial stretch of water with a wooded island fringed with reeds and tall trees that was created in 1818 by John Dobson as part of the grounds of the Georgian mansion of Bolam Hall.

The woods in the park are a stronghold of the red squirrel's, and a delightful spot for a family picnic. The lake offers the opportunity for paddling, boating and fishing. Nearby St Andrews church has a west tower that dates from the late Saxon period. A fourteenth century effigy is thought to be that of Robert de Reymes who built Aydon castle.

In World War II, in an attempt to escape from British fighters, a German pilot jettisoned three bombs. One landed and exploded in the front garden of the rectory where the crater now forms a bowl-shaped depression in the lawn, a second bomb went through the church's roof but failed to explode. A third landed northeast of the church and the explosion formed a crater, which is now a duck pond!

To the south can be seen the tower of Shortflatt a good example of a fourteenth century pele tower with modern additions. Shortflatt was also owned by Robert de Reymes and in the thirteenth century he received permission to crenellate both houses and as a result they are similar in their style and internal arrangements. Aydon developed more into a miniature fortress whereas Shortflatt does not present so many military features.

To the north lies another nature reserve, that of Hartburn Glebe Wood, perched on the south bank of the Hart. This was also the sight where the Roman road, The Devils Causeway, crossed the river and in the nineteenth century evidence was found of a timber bridge, the only one known along its route.

Bolam Lake Country Park

Harvest time near Bywell

BRAYDON CRAGS

Its hard to imagine that all of the isolated rock outcrops we see, such as Braydon Crags over looking the College Valley, are all that is left of a complete layer of rock possibly hundreds of kilometres long and several metres thick.

Over millions of years the wind, sun, rain and ice have worn the rock away until all that is left above ground are these few remnants, rather crumbs, on a plate. These forces also acted on the valley itself. The College Valley is part of the Northumberland National Park and is one of England's best-kept secrets. What keeps The College so beautiful and unspoilt is that although open to walkers, providing they keep to the footpaths, only twelve cars a day are allowed up into it and during the lambing season no cars are permitted whatsoever.

Formed by a geological fault some three million years ago, it was later gauged out by a glacier flowing from the top of The Cheviot which gives its high sided hills that characteristic U-shape. The meltwater from the smaller glaciers flowing off the hill summits deposited pebbles and sand along the valley floor which can be seen as gravel terraces left above the course of The College Burn.

The Cheviot feral goats, descendants of the domesticated goats of Iron Age hill farmers, roam these hills, their huge horns remind one of ibex as they seem to leap effortlessly from crag to crag.

Outside the village hall that serves as a gathering place for the valley's inhabitants is a circular

Braydon Crags, College Valley

memorial to the aircrews of various nations who lost their lives during the Second World War when training for low level missions or who crashed on the hills when returning home.

Nearby is the Hen Hole, a steep gorge with over twenty waterfalls cascading and bubbling down its length. Legends abound about this place, fairies lived in the mossy clefts, huntsmen were lured to

their deaths by mysterious music, and Black Adam, a renowned Border raider, had his lair high up the gorge. It is said that at a wedding in Wooperton he robbed the guests and stabbed the bride. Pursued by the bridegroom they both attempted to jump the gorge, slipped, and died on the rocks below.

DOD LAW & LOW HUMBLETON

Lying on the southern rim of Doddington Moor is one of the most concentrated areas of prehistoric rock art. The old shepherd's hut at Dodd Law has some of the most magnificent views in Northumberland. Dodd Law itself is a hill fort, a defensive site at the scarp edge, the walls of which cover some examples of rock art thus showing that the cup and ring marks are of a far earlier time than the Iron Age hill forts.

Behind is the valley of the River Glen or Glendale, as it was known, and to the left the mass of Humbelton Hill.

Standing at the north east corner of the Cheviots, Humbelton too has a hill fort on its peak with its ramparts still visible. When built around 2000 years ago this wall was probably some 2 metres high and 3 metres thick.

Throughout the ages Humbleton has been pronounced and spelt differently but all the variations are derived from the old English name for Cleft Hill, after the deep ravine to the south that separates the hill from the mass of the Cheviots. It is thought that this ravine was formed by meltwater scouring it out when the great ice sheets covered the hills.

In 1402 it was known as Homildon Hill and in this year a battle mentioned in Shakespeare's play 'Henry IV part 1' took place here. The Scottish army had laid siege to Newcastle upon Tyne and

Dod Law

were camped with their booty on the hill, whilst Hotspur occupied Harehope Hill opposite and ordered his archers to pour volley after volley into the close packed Scottish ranks clustered about their plunder laden wagons.

They had no choice but to make for the lower land and scatter where the English cavalry harried them ruthlessly. As was the way with so many

medieval battles more were killed in the pursuit than on the actual battlefield.

The site where most of the fleeing soldiers made their last stand can be identified just south of Bendor in a field off the A697 where today the solitary Bendor Stone can be seen rising from the fields of summer swaying wheat.

DUDDO STONE CIRCLE

Duddo Stone Circle

North Northumberland was one of the most active and culturally rich areas of the country in the Neolithic and Bronze Ages. Particularly evident are henges, a circular monument usually formed by an outer earth mound and inner ditch with one or two entrances. The other evidence is found in stone circles consisting of a ring of standing stones, although some had timber posts, set in a circular pattern.

The Millfield Plain is particularly rich in Neolithic monuments and excavations and aerial photography just south of Milfield have given further light on a monument known as the Coupland Enclosure. A massive circular earthwork which also shows signs of a large droveway and enclosure and is thought to date to about 3,700 BC, which would make it, the earliest henge related monument yet found.

Fifteen henge like structures have been noted in the area but the most visible monument still surviving are the Duddo Stones.

The Duddo Stone Circle consists of stones with their bases narrowed and smoothed. It is thought it may have been built to mark a cremation burial in the centre as the stone settings are much smaller that those circles which were meeting places or religious centres.

Other remains of circles exist in the county, one of the largest being Threestone Burn near Ilderton. This oval stone ring measures approximately over 30 metres by 29 metres and was made up of 13 stones of which only 5 remain. The tallest stone measures around 2 metres high and can be found on the north side.

The hamlet of Duddo also has a large tower that is perched on a prominent mound overlooking the surrounding countryside. Now a ruin, it was destroyed by the Scots before the battle of Flodden but from the architecture it would appear to have been restored around the reign of Elizabeth. The tower has also suffered from subsidence due to the coal workings underneath it.

KIELDER

Kielder

Kielder's modern history starts in 1775 when the castle was built as a shooting lodge for the Duke of Northumberland. However, it is the reservoir and forest that are brought to mind when the name is mentioned.

Kielder still is an isolated region but in the eighteenth century it was even more so. In fact Sir Walter Scott noted in his journal that 'The Duke tells me his people were all quite wild the first time his father went up to shoot up there'. There are records of a strange dance being performed here too when the women chanted and the men took part in a form of war dance brandishing the dirks they always wore.

Kielder Water is Northern Europe's largest man-made lake, cradled within the huge Kielder Forest Park. The lake holds a staggering 200 billion litres of water to supply the people and industries of the North East making sure they always have enough for their needs.

At the same time Kielder, with over 150 million trees, is the largest forest in England and one of the largest man-made forests in Europe. Covering an area of 62,000 hectares of which four fifths - 50,000 hectares, are planted in one large unit.

Sitka spruce is the main species at in the forest and is the tree that thrives best in this hostile upland environment, accounting for three quarters of the forest area.

Both the lake and forest provide shelter and food to endangered species. In particular the red squirrel thrives here and recently the osprey has returned and bred successfully.

Feeding the reservoir, and almost reaching into Scotland, are the Deadwater and White Kielder Burns but when the water leaves the lake it becomes the North Tyne. Before it reaches Bellingham it is joined by the Tarset and the Rede, names that are evocative of the most turbulent times of Borders history and showing that this area suffered more than most.

THE NORTH PENNINES

The North Pennines are called 'England's last Wilderness', a point that is best exemplified by the fact that in places they make the Cheviots seem positively well populated! The area was the centre of the county's lead mining industry and the only two settlements of any size are Allendale Town and Allenheads.

Within Northumberland's borders, to the east they are bordered by the picturesque village of Blanchland, Slaley Forest and the Derwent Reservoir and from here they sweep westwards in a bleak, almost desolate swathe until they reach the Cumbrian border above Alston.

There are three main valleys of the North Pennines in Northumberland. South Tynedale which ends at Haltwhistle, Allendale which joins the Tyne to the west of Haydon Bridge and the Derwent Valley which forms part of the border with County Durham.

Places such as Knarsdale, Slaggyford and Ninebanks tend to hug the roads in the sheltered valleys, those roads that are on the tops of the hills are amongst the highest in the county, whilst steep sided valleys such as Swinhope Burn to the West of Allenheads are littered with disused mine shafts and buildings. Most of the villages in the area have strong connections to the days of the lead mining industry and old mine chimneys still dot the landscape.

The area is one of England's largest 'Areas of

The North Pennines

Outstanding Natural Beauty', where gentle river valleys are found nestling between the rolling hills and rugged moors. Curlew, Merlin, Peregrines, Red Grouse and England's largest population of the Black Grouse may also be seen regularly in this great heather moorland.

This is an area where what impresses one most is the almost total lack of woods and forestry plantations in what seems a direct contrast to the other upland parts of the county. Only in the valleys and on the lower slopes will you find the sheltering blocks of timber whilst the high areas of Whitley and Knaresdale Common have a stark beauty that is all their own.

ROUGHTING LINN

Northumberland is the most prolific and important area for the rock art known as cup-and-ring markings in Britain with 500 examples still existing and at around 3000 years old Roughting Linn is the largest carved outcrop in Northern England.

The name Roughting Linn comes from the nearby waterfall being 'Linn' a pool and 'Roughting' a bellowing noise. The rock was originally much bigger and must have been an impressive site but the western part was quarried away around 1850 and a large slab has also been removed across its width. Stan Beckinsall regards it as 'One of the most important pieces of rock art in the world'.

These carvings in stone consist of an inner 'cup', actually a hemispherical depression surround by rings. Sometimes there is a duct connecting the cup with the outside of the rings. They were originally carved on sandstone during the Neolithic period and were later incorporated into burial cairns and stone circles. Some can be found at Morwick on a cliff face near a fording place on the Coquet.

Excellent examples occur at Lordenshaws and Doddington Moor, and stumbling across them on walks is very common. The significance of these amazingly detailed carvings is still not known, but it may have been that they conveyed messages about tribal boundaries, represented spiritual beliefs or were some form of boundary marker.

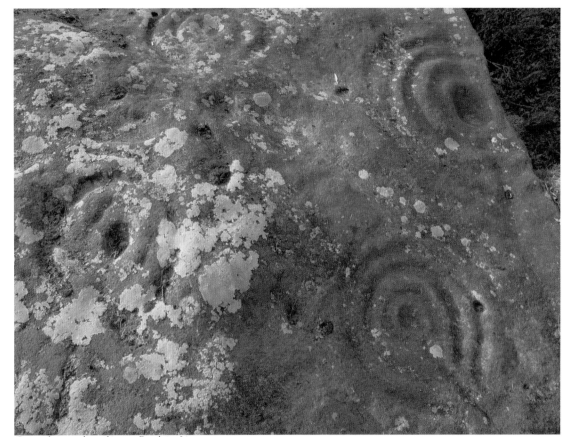
Cup and ring rock markings at Roughting Linn

It is possible, especially in low light, to see the individual marks from the picks that produced the designs. A variety of tools must have been used with different head widths from fine flint like points to broader ones similar to modern chisels.

Most of the carvings are in relatively soft rock. Therefore, it is safe to assume that something such as andesite or whinstone could have been used probably with the use of a mallet. However, as of yet no definite tools have been found. The nearest archaeologists have come to this is at Dod Law, where a pick was found close to peck marks on a rock that had been covered by a later Iron Age structure.

UPPER COQUETDALE

Upper Coquetdale is in all respects of the phrase a truly magnificent wilderness. You only have to visit it once and experience the brooding hills unfolding around the road as it follows the twists and turns of the river for it to be eternally etched in your memory.

Harbottle is the start of the valley with its ruined castle where the grandmother of James VI of Scotland and I of England was born. Above the village is the proud, lonely Drake Stone nearly ten metres high where sick children were once passed over it to be cured.

A few miles up the valley where the Coquet meets the Alwin is the village of Alwinton, now famous for its annual Border Shepherds show which is one of the last of the many agricultural shows that are held across the region throughout the year. Heading north out of the village is Clennel Street, one of the great ancient droving roads that heads northwards to the border.

As you follow the Coquet northwards the valley sides hem in looming over you with Shillope law and Dumb Hope towering above. This is the land of birds rarely seen in the lowlands such as the dipper, merlin and the ring ouzel.

It is also the land of the military, as today it is used by the army as part of their Otterburn military training area. Here troops from all over Europe can be seen marching along the roads, whilst armoured vehicles and low flying aircraft disturb the everyday

Upper Coquetdale

silence of the wilderness.

However these modern examples of the face of warfare that has straddled this land for centuries will ensure that it remains a desolate place, even though the roar of Land Rovers and army trucks sometimes break the ancient stillness.

This land is also where the stell is seen. These dry

stone circular walls are built in sheltered places where the sheep can be gathered in severe weather for lambing. They are also used by walkers and soldiers seeking a quiet sheltered place to make a cup of tea and hide from the penetrating winds of the upper moorlands.

Warkworth beach

Corbridge

Northumberland

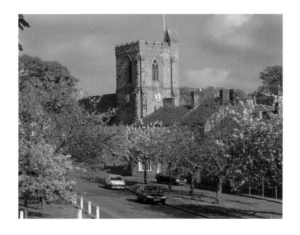

MARKET TOWNS AND VILLAGES

MARKET TOWNS AND VILLAGES

The towns and villages of Northumberland are a treasure trove in their own right. It would take another book the size of this to cover all of the fascinating, hidden delights that are to be found in their streets. How many of us for example know of Beltingham, with its stone-roofed cottages clustered around a tiny green where the River Allen meets the South Tyne?

Because of the difference in the landscape from high moorland to industrial hinterland the communities that have developed are vastly different. Some recognisable towns only developed in the nineteenth century with the coming of coal, Ashington, Linton, Allendale and Amble are cases in point.

With the Industrial Revolution neighbouring small villages such as Old Hartley and Seaton Sluice gradually melded together. In the twentieth century the new town of Cramlington swallowed Nelson, and Cowpen and Newsham became effectively part of Blyth.

The great coaching days brought prosperity to places such as Morpeth, Felton, Alnwick and Belford whilst other coaching inns can be found at Corbridge and Haltwhistle. Along with Haltwhistle's claim to be the geographical centre of Britain it can also claim to have more fortified houses than any town in the country.

Sir Walter Scott was a frequent visitor to Alnwinton. Bedlington, the capital of Bedlingtonshire until 1844 when it was incorporated in to Northumberland, is now best known for the famous breed of terrier which originated here.

The market town was the hub of Northumberland life for centuries drawing in people from the surrounding villages to sell their animals and buy their provisions. In towns such as Rothbury, Hexham and Wooler this is still very much the case and indeed Bellingham, Haltwhistle, Alnwick, Morpeth and Otterburn also act in this way to a lesser extent.

Many of the villages have changed little since the nineteenth century with most still having stone walls and slate roofs. Once thatch was common in many parts of Northumberland but now is restricted to Etal village which also has some amazingly large Welsh slates on some of it houses. So big are they in fact that the largest ones are 4cm thick and weigh 25kg each. To accommodate so much weight, the roof trusses of the buildings are specially reinforced and the whole pitch of the roof is somewhat steeper than normal.

Some of the most isolated communities are found in the valley of the South Tyne and on the North Pennine moors, but when the deep snow comes the

Forestry villages like Kielder, Byrness, and other communities in the Cheviots can become cut off.

On the coast villages such as Low Newton and Craster still bear witness of the fishing past whilst other have grown up in the shadow of castles and grand homes such as Chillingham, Warkworth and Cambo. Some, like Belsay, have been forcibly moved to a new site due to the landscaping of the great estates whilst a similar fate has occurred at Hadston due to mining.

Before the coming of the mining industry some places such as Ashington and Amble simply did not exist as we now know them. Others have been altered deliberately to accommodate the tourist industry. The amusement arcades and gift shops of Seahouses are clustered in one place while other coastal villages remain virtually unaltered.

Rochester, Allenheads, Alnmouth, Milfield and others have seen the springing up of tourist related industries and in many of our villages bed & breakfast and holiday cottage accommodation is rapidly becoming greater than residential homes. Yet despite this peaceful oasis of tranquillity still survive. Norham and Blanchland may be at opposite ends of the county but they both epitomise what is so wonderful about the Northumberland village.

Opposite: Wooler, 'The Gateway to the Cheviots'

ALNWICK MARKET PLACE

The Market in Alnwick dates back to the 1200s and over this period of time it has had a series of market crosses. The current Market cross is known as the 'Town Cross' the place for proclamations to townspeople.

The buildings surrounding the square show a fascinating range of architectural design and age and the Town Hall, built in 1771, is not owned by the council but by the freemen of Alnwick.

Stretching along the south side of the square and constructed in 1826 by the third Duke of Northumberland for use as assembly rooms is The Northumberland Hall, it was presented as a gift to the people of Alnwick by a later Duke.

Beneath the Northumberland Hall are the Shambles, where butcher's shops once stood and the eastern end of it is still called the fish market by some inhabitants today.

A weekly market has been held in the square for over 800 years and today the market is held twice a week, on Thursdays and Saturdays. The square is also the centre of Alnwick's activities in the summer when the Medieval Faire, (first started in 1297), International Music Festival and the Northumbrian Gathering are held.

The square has had a chequered history serving as a bus station in 1930s and as a car park for much of the later part of the twentieth century. Occasionally at 8 o'clock at night the curfew bell is rung out 20 times across the square from the town hall as it has been for centuries.

Running off the Market Place in each corner to the North are two narrow lanes that lead in to Narrowgate one of the oldest parts of the town whilst to the south two broad openings either side of The Northumberland Hall bring you out onto the broad vista of the cobbles opposite, with St Michael's Pant looking down the street to the Bondgate Arch.

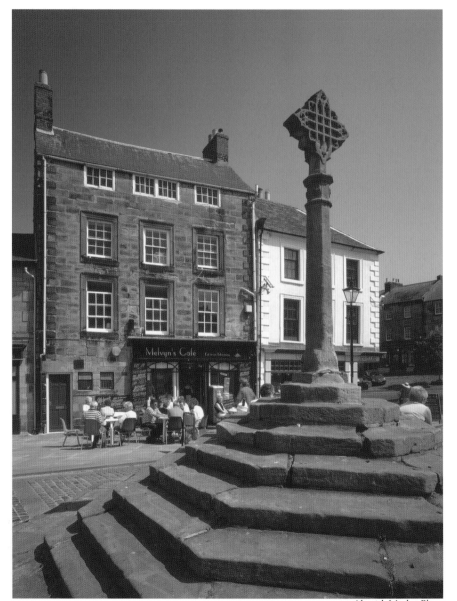

Alnwick Market Place

BELFORD

The Great North Road was instrumental in bringing prosperity to a number of villages along its route and Belford was no exception. The Blue Bell Hotel in the market place, still with its original market cross standing on three steps, was an important staging post for the coaches as they travelled between Edinburgh and London.

Margaret Tudor, daughter of King Henry VII, was recorded as having stayed in the village on her progress north to marry James IV of Scotland in 1502.

In 1636 the village was described as 'the most miserable beggarly sodden town, or town of sods that ever was made in an afternoon of loam and sticks'.

To the east of the village is Belford Hall, owned in the late nineteenth century by George Dixon Atkinson Clark, the chief landowner. The hall was built in the 1750s by Abraham Dixon and some of its features are from later designs of the architect James Paine.

The Hall was later enlarged by John Dobson and it remains a very good example of an eighteenth century mansion house set in parkland with estate cottages and housing still bearing Dobson's mark evident in the village.

The east end of St Mary's church was originally a chapel exclusively for the use of the owners of the Hall. The present building was rebuilt by Dobson

in 1828 and in the churchyard is an interesting single storied building with bars on the windows to deter bodysnatchers.

To the north of the village is the old mansion of Middleton Hall with its lakes and rhododendrons. The houses were lit by a hydroelectrical system using the water from the three lakes, and there is actually some dispute as to whether it was here or Cragside that saw the world's first use of this power.

Belford Hall and St Mary's Church, Belford

BERWICK UPON TWEED

There is probably no other town in Britain that has had such a long and violent history as Berwick. The town's location in the Borders made it a strategic target in the endless wars between the English and the Scots and as a result changed hands no less than thirteen times over a period of 300 years.

In 1603, when James VI of Scotland was crowned James I of England, the conflict between the two nations ceased. Berwick was the first English town visited by James on his way south to London, and the following year the King granted a new charter for the Borough.

Inside the Elizabethan walls Berwick has a host of treasures for the visitor. On Hyde Hill is the King's Arms Hotel, one of the great coaching inns where Charles Dickens stayed on many occasions. Tucked away behind the walls on the south side of the town is the old heart of Berwick where the Governor's Palace still stands in a leafy square, whilst ships' figureheads thrust themselves out from house walls.

The maritime history is shown further along, just to the north, in a long lawn called The Avenue. This area was originally used by the town's rope factory to lay out their new ropes in order to let them dry. The granaries around Dewers Lane still stand, and at Bankside and Ravendowne the ice houses, where ice for the salmon trade was stored, can still be seen.

As Berwick was a major port it suffered from its

Berwick upon Tweed

fair share of crime and alongside the wall of the ancient Town Hall, the town stocks can still be seen.

The Town Hall also has a covered Buttermarket and a handsome balustrade runs around the roof where the prisoners, from the still existing cells below, were exercised.

The Town Hall also houses the bells of Berwick's parish church which is one of only two churches in the country dating from the time of the Commonwealth under the rule of Cromwell.

BERWICK TOWN WALLS

There are actually two sets of town walls at Berwick. The first, of which little remains, were built by Edward II and were just over two miles long. The tall octagonal bell tower on the north side was one of Edward's nineteen towers and acted as a bell and beacon warning station if an enemy force was seen approaching.

In 1558 Queen Mary Tudor ordered Sir Richard Lee to Berwick to strengthen the medieval town walls against further attacks by the Scots. When Mary died she was succeeded by her sister Elizabeth and the need for the completion of the walls became even more urgent.

Still known today as the 'Elizabethan Walls' they are the finest preserved late medieval walls in Europe and a walk round them brings you face to face with the towns turbulent history.

The houses on the walls above the old quayside have large cellars beneath them and if you descend to the Quayside below you'll see huge doors cut into the wall by the merchants who owned the houses above. Small lanes run off the walls and it's worthwhile exploring them as here you'll find the huge warehouses and factories where the shoes that supplied over half the country in the eighteenth century were made.

A little further on is the Sand Gate where once the sea lapped up to its walls and further on the Custom House still stands and looks down on the old heart of Berwick

Berwick Town Walls

Where the walls face due south are a row of grand houses. The first of these has harpoons carved above the door showing it was built for a whaler and a truly magnificent vista now opens up before you. To the south you can see Lindisfarne with its castle perched high above the island and behind, a few miles to the south, the brooding mass of Bamburgh castle.

The walls near the barracks have the powder magazine just behind them and the eastern gate into the town. It is the only original one still standing and is known as Cowgate because up until the 1950s farmers brought their cattle in through it on their way to the market.

BLANCHLAND

Blanchland

Nestling right on the border with County Durham, Blanchland has been called one of the most perfect villages of England. There would be very few travellers who, driving down from the wild, deserted moorland surrounding the village into the wooded glen of the Derwent, would dispute this description.

A small, isolated community in the upper reaches of the Derwent Valley it is thought that the name, which means 'white land' comes from the white habits that the Premonstratensian monks wore.

Blanchland Abbey was founded in 1165 on land given to twelve monks of the order by Walter de Bolbec. The house was more than once burnt by the Scots but quite a lot of the abbey buildings still remain.

Included amongst these is the eighteenth century church, dramatically rebuilt in the eighteenth and nineteenth centuries. The churchyard cross still remains with its traceried head, a very rare survival, looking much as it probably did when John Wesley preached here in the churchyard in 1747.

The fifteenth century monastery gatehouse has also survived whilst the west range of the cloister is now part of the Lord Crewe Arms Hotel.

After the Dissolution the estate fell into decline. It was first owned by the Radcliffes and then bought in 1623 by the Forsters of Bamburgh. In 1699 Dorothy Forster married Lord Crewe, Bishop of Durham who bought the debt-ridden estate in 1704. When Lord Crewe died he left his estates to trustees with the income to go to various schools and almshouses.

The Lord Crewe Arms is reputed to be haunted by the ghost of Dorothy Forster niece to the Bishop of Durham and Lady Crewe and sister to Tom Forster who was captured during 1715 Jacobite Rebellion.

Taken to London and imprisoned in Newgate gaol he managed to escape three days before he was due to stand trial for high treason. The escape was planned by his sister Dorothy, then aged 11, who disguised herself as his servant, rode to London behind the village blacksmith and made good her brother's escape.

CAMBO

The village of Cambo was first laid out as a model village in 1740, set off from the main road resulting in a quiet and secluded area. The village itself is sheltered and the buildings are set within groups of mature trees that provide an effective screen to views from the open countryside and approach roads.

The old schoolhouse, altered and enlarged by Sir George Otto Trevelyan in 1911, was the site of Lancelot 'Capability' Brown's, who was born at nearby Kirkharle, early education and he returned later in life to assist in developing the grounds at Wallington Hall.

The village layout is of terraced cottages enclosing a square that consists of a walled green and several very attractive walled private gardens. The predominant use of ashlar stonework gives a pleasing conformity to the buildings of the village.

An early chapel here dating from the twelfth to the fifteenth Century was demolished in 1875, a few coffin lids were preserved and are now set in the walls of the present building, inside, opposite the main entrance. The church we see today was consecrated in 1842 and was built by Sir John Trevelyan of Wallington Hall and in the churchyard lie several members of the Trevelyan family.

Sir Charles Trevelyan added the tower to the church and presented it with a clock and bells. He also rebuilt the present roof with floral bosses and coloured coats of arms. Four windows added as

Cambo Village

family memorials and the window in the tower were added by Sir Charles' widow, a sister of Macaulay. The village is now in the care of the National Trust.

To the west is the quiet village of Kirkwhelpington situated at the foot of the wild moors that climb away to the Cheviots with its thirteenth century church that was once much larger. Buried in the churchyard is Sir Charles Parsons the inventor of the steam turbine which brought about a transformation in steam power.

ETAL VILLAGE

Any visitor to Etal village cannot possibly be untouched by its charm. However to many visitors the village's character comes from its curious mixture of architectural styles, stone slate side by side with thatch and whitewash next to sandstone. Indeed, 'The Black Bull' is Northumberland's only thatched pub. Whereas once thatching was common throughout north Northumberland, the buildings of Etal are virtually all that remain.

Some of the slates used on the whitewashed house's roofs are of far larger size than normal and they are probably an unusual Welsh slate (rather than Westmorland). The largest ones (at the bottom) are an inch and half thick and weigh 55lbs each! To accommodate so much weight, the roof trusses of the buildings are specially reinforced and the whole pitch of the roof is somewhat steeper than normal.

The village is sandwiched between the large manor house at one end of the village and the remains of the castle at the other thus gives Etal its own distinctive aspect among the county's villages. The Manor house was built for Sir William Carr in 1748 and enlarged a few years later and then passed in to the hands of the Joicey family when they purchased the estate in 1908. In its grounds stand the red-banded rubbled walls of the church of the Blessed Virgin Mary in which the villagers have worshipped since the middle of the nineteenth century.

The church was designed by William Butterfield in 1850 and in the middle of the roof is a turret for two bells. The church was given by Lady Augusta Fitzclarence in memory of her husband (Lord Frederic Fitzclarence, who died in 1855, one of the ten children of William IV and Mrs Jordan) and their only child, Augusta Georgina, who survived her father by only few months.

In nearby Crookham, just across the Till, the Crookham Affray took place in 1678, it turned out to be the last skirmish of the border wars fought between the Scots and English.

Etal Village

FORD

Ford village as seen today is the work of Lady Louisa Waterford, who developed it as a memorial to her husband who suffered a fatal fall from a horse in 1859. The original village was to the west of the castle under, what was then, the main entrance.

As a bridesmaid of Queen Victoria, Lady Waterford was highly thought of by nineteenth century Northumberland society. She was also an artist of no mean talent and during her long widowhood she decorated the halls of the village school, which she also had built, with a remarkable series of murals.

Lady Waterford painted these murals between 1862 and 1883 using pupils from the school and people from the surrounding area as her models. These and other works by her are on display in the building which remained a school until 1957. The murals possess a wonderful sense of deep colour and the wooden beamed ceiling gives a further marvellous effect

Lady Waterford lived in Ford Castle, now owned by Lord Joicey and used as a county educational and cultural centre. The castle was first built in 1287 by Odenel de Forde and crenellated in 1338. It was in the style of four corner towers with a curtain-wall, and three of these original towers still survive.

It was destroyed by the Scots in 1385 and badly burnt before the Battle of Flodden. Again in 1549 it was put under siege by heavy cannon but managed to hold out. The castle was extensively restored in the gothic style in 1761 by John Delaval, and again in the nineteenth century by Lady Waterford.

St Michael's church in the castle grounds is early thirteenth century with a thorough nineteenth century restoration. Its massive bell turret is of a rare type, with a pyramidal cap and window like openings for the bells. The old smithy in the village must surely have one of the largest advertising signs anywhere in the country.

The Smithy, Ford Village

MATFEN

There are many great families who have influenced Northumberland's history. Names such as Percy, Trevelyan, Grey and Heron all ring out clear down the ages but one the most important, certainly in the case of Newcastle and its surroundings, was that of Blackett.

The Gothic style Matfen Hall has been the home of the Blackett family since 1830. It incorporates two earlier houses, one medieval, and the other dating from 1685 and was built by Sir Edward Blackett, the sixth Baronet. In 1961 The Hall became a Cheshire Home for the next thirty years. In 1999 the Hall was restored and transformed into a luxury hotel by Sir Hugh and Lady Blackett.

Behind the hall lies the pleasant village of Matfen with its green lined with sycamores and a bubbling stream adding to its character. Matfen church was built in the early Victorian period in 1842 and was consecrated on 17 September 1844. The church was built at the expense of Sir Edward Blackett, Bart, of Matfen Hall. Matfen was then part of Stamfordham parish.

The Romans too were here as Matfen is just to the north of the wall and the round umbo of the shield of a legionary, serving in the century of Ruspus Quintus was found here.

A far older relic is to be found in The Matfen Standing Stone opposite a farm named after it but there is some thought that it may have been moved from its original position. On three sides of its base,

Matfen

close to the ground, are many examples of prehistoric rock art in the form of cup marks.

To the south, near the site of what was Milecastle 18, the Vallum of Hadrian's Wall is in a particularly good state of repair here. Gaps in the north and south mounds and causeways in the ditch can still be seen as the Roman engineers designed them. They provided the original crossing places for any travellers passing through.

MORPETH

One of the most amazing things about Northumberland is how many people who have changed the world have connections here. The exact effect of the suffragette Emily Davison being killed by the Kings Horse in the 1913 Derby on women getting the vote may be open to debate, but her grave in Morpeth is constantly visited.

The castle at Morpeth does not ring loudly in history. In 1138 Ranulph de Merlay entertained the eight monks who were to found the monastery at Newminster. The castle was burnt by King John and suffered a terrible siege of cannon during the civil war.

Morpeth's buildings are of some note, the clock tower is one of only three built during the medieval period and from where the night curfew rang out at 8 o'clock every evening. The Town Hall was designed by Vanburgh and Collingwood House in Oldgate Street was the home of Admiral Collingwood, Nelson's second in command at Trafalgar.

The fine bridge built by Thomas Telford between 1829–31 and its inns such as The Black Bull and the Queens Head, which has a truly magnificent coloured heraldic fireplace bearing the date 1656, shows the town's links with the coaching period.

By the side of the bridge is a block of buildings that are relics of the thirteenth century chantry chapel of All Saints where the tolls were collected.

Morpeth town. Below right: The Clock Tower

Today the Chantry combines a unique Bagpipe Museum with the Northumbrian Craft Centre.

The old bridge over the Wansbeck was destroyed in 1832 and was so narrow and steep that on two occasions the mail coach knocked away the parapets and fell into the river.

One of Northumberland's major market towns and the administrative centre for the County Council, the town is still a bustling place and recently has required a reputation for its night life with a variety of restaurants and places of entertainment.

PRUDHOE

Prudhoe Castle

Prudhoe means 'proud hill' and lying on the south bank of the Tyne the town is linked by the narrow toll bridge that was built in 1883 to replace the old ferry that ran across to Ovingham.

Apart from a small amount of Bronze Age data, not much is known about the pre Norman history of the town that is dominated by the castle built in the twelfth century by Odinel de Umfreville.

Twice in its history, 1173 and 1174, William the Lion of Scotland besieged the castle. The castle remained a fortress of the Umfrevilles until 1381 then passed to the Percys. After the Union of the Crowns the castle fell into disuse and is now in the in the care of English Heritage.

In the last quarter of the nineteenth century Matthew Liddell started mining for coal in the area and to support this brickworks at Mickley and Edgewell and Clay Pipe works at Eltringham were constructed.

These industries befitted the Liddell family and within a few years they were able to build Prudhoe Hall. Almost 100 years ago the church of Our Lady & St. Cuthbert was dismantled and transferred on hand carts by the local community from the hall to its present site.

The Prudhoe Gleemen is one of the oldest and most famous Male Voice choirs in the North East of England. The Choir was founded in 1903 and is still delighting audiences all over the country with its excellent and varied singing.

Across the river is the quiet village of Ovingham with it seventeenth century packhorse bridge with two sturdy arches that straddles the Whittle Burn where once linen was bleached.

The church of St Mary has a Saxon tower and in its porch a young Thomas Bewick would while away the hours with chalk drawings of animals and birds.

Each year on the third Saturday in June the Ovingham Goose Fair takes place, a traditional village fair with morris and country dancing, crafts and Northumbrian pipes. A procession leaves the Goose Fair Cross and walks to the Pack Horse Bridge for the proclamation to be read at the start of the Fair.

ROTHBURY

Rothbury is an ancient barony, and from 1095 it was held by the crown. It passed through various owners before coming into the hands of the Percy family in the 1330s.

The bridge at Rothbury crossing the Coquet dates from the fifteenth century, originally it was a three arch pack horse bridge with a fourth arch being added in the eighteenth century as the river widened and the road became more important. This road became the corn road from Hexham to the port at Alnmouth and is still historically significant today as it is along its route that many of Northumberland's milestones still survive.

Originally the bridge had a toll cottage a few hundred yards to the south, on the Hexham road.

Known as the 'Capital of Coquetdale', Rothbury is a small, quiet town with its sloping green shaded by sycamores. However it is in the shadow of the house at Cragside and the influence of the Armstrong family is all around.

The present Market Cross was erected in 1902 as a mark of admiration and remembrance for Lord and Lady Armstrong of Cragside and replaced the earlier one which was falling down. To the east of the village Lord Armstrong erected a block of twelve cottages in 1896 that are still standing today and look as pristine as the day they were built. Originally known as Almshouses they were established as homes for aged estate workers.

To the south, the town is dominated by the

Rothbury

Simonside Hills, now very popular with walkers and weekend visitors. Perched on the side of the hills is Great Tosson which can be visited by walking over the footbridge above Rothbury.

The pele tower here was part of the defensive line of towers and castle along the Coquet valley and when Hepple Tower was destroyed, probably by Robert the Bruce, the Lords of Hepple held court here.

Abutting on the Simonside Hill is the wonderful and varied landscape of Lordenshaws with its ancient cup and ring rock art, huge Iron Age hillfort and medieval field system.

Alnmouth

BIBLIOGRAPHY

Archaeology in the Northumberland National Park, Paul Frodsham (C.B.A. 2004)

A Fortified Frontier, Iain MacIvor (Tempus 2001)

A Journey Through Northumberland, Clive Crossley - Graeme Peaock (Northumberland 2002)

Borderland Castles & Peles, R.Hugill (Sandhill Press 1996)

From Blyth to Berwick and Back, H.G. Dobson (H.G.Dobson 2002)

Ghost Trails of Northumberland, Clive Kristen (Casdec 1992)

Hartley to Seaton Sluice, The Military Connection, David. J. Anderson (Seaton Design 1999)

Historic Sites of Northumberland & Newcastle upon Tyne, G.L.Dodds (Albion Press 2002)

History of Northumberland, Cadwallader J. Bates (Sandhill Press 1996)

Industrial Archaeology of North East England, F.Atkinson (David & Charles 1974)

Land of Legend, Clive Waddington, (Country Store Publishing 1999)

Lindisfarne, the Cradle Island, M.Magnusson

Northumberland Coastline I. Smith (Sandhill Press 1999)

Northumbria, L. Frost (Constable 2001)

Northumbria, English Border Country, Talbot & Whiteman (Wiedenfield & Nicholson 1998)

Northumbria's Golden Age, Hawkes & Mills (Sutton Publishing 1999)

Prehistoric Rock Art in Northumberland, S.Beckensall (Tempus 2001)

Roman Frontiers of Britain, D.R.Wilson (Heinmann 1967)

'The Bonny Fisher Lad', Katrina Porteous (The People's History 2003)

The Kingdom of Northumbria AD 350-1100, N.J. Higham (Alan Sutton 1993)

The Kings England, Northumberland, Arthur Mee (Hodder & Stoughton 1969)

The Ship That Came Home, A.W. Purdoe (Third Millenium 2004)

Upper North Tynedale, Beryl Charlton (Northumbria Water 1987)

INDEX